SEEN

*Experiencing God's
Tenderness After Brokenness*

by
REBECCA MEDINA STEWART

Published by hope*books
2217 Matthews Township Pkwy
Suite D302
Matthews, NC 28105
www.hopebooks.com

hope*books is a division of hope*media

Printed in the United States of America

First edition.

Paperback ISBN: 979-8-89185-207-5
Hardcover ISBN: 979-8-89185-124-5
Ebook ISBN: 979-8-89185-125-2
Library of Congress Number: 2024945966

ENDORSEMENTS

"Rebecca Medina Stewart manages to show in so many different ways how God turns graves into gardens. Everything from her survival story of being sexually assaulted to people struggling with addiction to battling cancer. This devotional is unlike any I've read before and leveled up my personal walk with Jesus more than I could have ever imagined. A must-read whether you know God or are just starting to seek him or have never acknowledged him. A must-read for everyone! You will find peace that transcends all understanding."

— JULIE CHEN MOONVES,
CBS Journalist, Author of *But First, God,*
Host of *Big Brother*

"The miraculous power of God's restoration and peace in the face of trauma and abuse shines through the pages of Rebecca's book *SEEN.* For victims of abuse and people who are struggling, this book is a kind nudge, a gentle outstretched hand to hold to take those steps back into fellowship, grace, and the loving arms of the Father. I knew Rebecca as a passionate journalist and a colleague in TV news. Now, I know her as a confident Christian woman, restored and renewed, using her story as a healing tool and a testimony to change lives in the name of Christ."

— WALT MACIBORSKI,
Friend and Anchor CBS Austin News

"I love me some Rebecca Medina Stewart! We have been friends for over a decade through personal and communal hardships. This book in my life is like a fine wine to a connoisseur—valuable and satiated. A fine wine is only as good as the pressing and process it goes through. Rebecca has pressed and processed one of humanity's most challenging hardships. Now, through this book, she shares with all of us the overflowing goodness God poured into her glass! As a forty-two-year struggler of suicide and the founder of a no-suicide nonprofit, this book will be a hopeful and healing component of the free LifeBoxes we ship daily around the country. Between Rebecca's story and my story, I believe God is going to get the glory for many more rescue stories!"

— HEATHER PALACIOS,
Founder of *WONDHERFUL, INC a 501c3 non-profit dedicated to saving the lives of those who are struggling thru mental crisis.*

"During my 26 years as a pastor, I have met a lot of great people. Occasionally, you meet someone, and they quickly stand out. That would be the case for Rebecca and her husband, Brian. Serving alongside them for many years and seeing their hearts for making Jesus smile has been a joy.

I was excited when I found out Rebecca was writing *SEEN* and was honored to be asked to endorse her book. As I began reading, I quickly realized the words written in this book provide great insight into the precious heart of Christ. What I didn't fully realize is the impact it would have on my personal life as I navigate my own healing from past trauma.

I believe we all deal with complex issues, and whether yours is listed in this book or not, the principles of God's healing apply to them all. *SEEN* is a book that will bring you face to face with your pain and the healing powers of Jesus Christ. If you are facing difficulty in your life or walking alongside someone who is, this book is a must-read for you."

— PASTOR JOEY BAILEY,
former Care Ministries Pastor at Church by the Glades

To El Roi, The God who saw me, healed my brokenness, and forever changed my life.

I love you.

CONTENTS

PART 3: The Brokenness of Domestic Abuse, Abandonment, or Neglect

PART 4: The Brokenness of Addiction

PART 5: The Brokenness of Mental Health Challenges

PART 6: The Brokenness of A Life of Sin

PART 7: The Brokenness of Infirmity

PART 8: Hope and Healing in the Power of God

ACKNOWLEDGMENTS

SEEN would never have happened without my extraordinary husband, Brian. His tender nudge and godly leadership brought me face-to-face with God's purpose for my life. He models Ephesians 5:25 perfectly, "For husbands, this means love your wives, just as Christ loved the church. He gave up his life for her." I am so grateful that God preserved him just for me. Brian was my greatest encourager, transcriber, proofreader, and go-to for ideas. You are my partner in every way, and you will forever have my heart.

My mother and favorite prayer warrior, Mercedes, exemplifies an unwavering and passionate love for Christ. Her steadfast example has shown me that Jesus is indeed the answer to everything. Her boundless love has nurtured me throughout my life, and it was her prayers that helped lead me back home. What a blessing to be able to call her "mom." I love you, Mercedes.

To the woman who cared for me during some of my darkest days – my sister Vanessa Spector – thank you for never giving up on me or leaving my side. You, too, helped bring me back. You will forever be my soul-*seester*.

My dad, Pablo, always said I would write a book. His confidence in me is unwavering. I love you, Papi. To my brother Spector: I love your giant heart and dedication to our family. Thank you for helping me when I needed it most.

My second mother, Evelyn, has been telling me to write since I was a young woman. She is a spiritual giant in my life, my godmother, confidant, and wise counselor. I love you, Titi.

May every word I write help make this world a better place for the not-so-little loves of my life – Gabriel, Gavin, and Sascha. May you grow to become the fiercest servants of Christ our family has ever seen. Sascha, thank you for inspiring the title of Day Three!

Writing this book reminded me about the power of community. I thank God for my family of spiritual giants! Mario, Cookie, Raul, Lisa, and the rest of our crew, I am grateful for you. You spoke life into this project. I am blessed to do life with a holy team of Aarons and Hurs (Exodus 17:12-13).

I extend my deepest gratitude to my invaluable team of beta readers (Brian, Vanessa, Lisa, and Keyla) for your vital contributions to this book. Your keen eyes, thoughtful feedback, and unwavering support have been instrumental in shaping this work into its best version. Your dedication and enthusiasm have improved the manuscript and inspired me to push the boundaries of my creativity. Thank you for your time, honesty, and belief in this project. This book is as much yours as it is mine.

The team at hope*books Publishing served as mentors, coaches, and even therapists (on some days). Hope*books created a beautiful space for writers to write, learn, and connect while walking through the publishing journey. My team: Dr. Brian Dixon, Krissy Nelson, Hope Dover, and Kati Benton. Editing never felt so good, thanks to Abby McDonald, my developmental editor. The Holy Spirit only amplifies your skill, and I am so thankful for your hard work and gentle instruction. Finally, to my AMAZING inaugural author cohort, I love you all! We were strangers when we came together, grabbed each other's hands, laughed, and cried along this adventure. Now, we are family! (Cue the music.)

My Journey to You

I was a naive 18-year-old girl who left home with big dreams and plans for her future. I was the first in my strict Latino family to go to college, and all I wanted was freedom. I grew up in the church, but my hunger for fun and adventure led me down a prodigal's path. Just a few months into my newfound independence, I was sexually assaulted by a man who posed as a university student. That night of hell haunted me and left me battling deep depression, extreme loneliness, isolation, and profound shame. For a long time, I put on a brave and tough face for the world, but privately, my life was crumbling into emotional and spiritual darkness beyond the reach of those I love.

My family spent years praying for me, and my Heavenly Father was kind and patient in His pursuit of me. The enemy, on the other hand, was relentless and used my trauma to keep me in a dark abyss of despair where my soul felt trapped and adrift in the vast expanse of emptiness. I settled into the belief that I would never find solid ground. Satan had me convinced there was no rescue for me, and life would always be sad, dark, and painful. But in time, I learned Satan is the Master of Lies, and God never let me go.

Many years after that dreadful night and nearly two decades worth of my mother's prayers, I finally cried out to Jesus, and He answered ever so tenderly. God never condemned or rebuked me, which is what I expected. He only loved me gently, deeply, and completely. The more I learned about Him, the deeper I fell in love with Him. I discovered a church community that embraced me without judgment, and with each step of obedience I took, the Lord painstakingly collected another shard of glass from the broken vase of my life. He skillfully reassembled it into a beauty beyond my wildest imagination.

He was gazing at me the whole time. I was *seen* by the God of the Universe, and He healed, transformed, and restored my life. God draws near to His children when we call upon His name, and His only agenda is to display His love for us. Through Christian counseling, prayer, my amazing church, and living in obedience to our Father, I learned that He longs to guide and redeem us if only we let Him. After all, friends, God is a gentleman who respects our free will.

As I immersed myself in my church community, I found the courage to open up and share my experiences with others. Through this process, I felt the weight of shame gradually loosening its grip on my spirit. Reflecting on my journey, I've come to realize a profound truth: there is no turmoil in our lives too deep for God's healing touch. Consider this – even the Perfect Christ endured the agony of wrongful accusations, torture, betrayal, and humiliation. I believe part of the reason He endured such suffering was so He could relate to the worst of our human experiences. No one understands the depths of trauma and brokenness like the Son of Man. And in case you need a reminder, He continues to be in the business of restoring and healing.

This book is a collection of devotional stories about messy, fractured men and women who experienced the chain-breaking power of healing, transformation, and restoration through faith and hope in Jesus. Some were healed, and some recognize they live in a fallen world, and their cure awaits them in eternity. But they all live with the confidence that God's grace is sufficient, and when we are weak and in pain, He remains strong and able to help us through. Healed or not, there is hope because of who God is!

"I have told you all this so that you may have peace in me. Here on earth you will have many trials and sorrows. But take heart, because I have overcome the world" John 16:33 NLT.

Friend, the world is waging a war on our souls. I cannot turn a blind eye to all those who are lost and broken like I was. I have come alongside the Lord to write these stories in hopes that you will be inspired to take your next step toward Jesus and His promise of peace, healing, and redemption.

I am not a trained mental health expert – just a girl who was lost and intensely broken until I invited God into my pain. He rescued me and radically changed my life. It was slow and sometimes very painful, but my loving Father has held me throughout this difficult journey.

In my research for this book, I interviewed founder and CEO of The Miranda Healing Group, Dr. Nadia Jimenez, PhD, LCSW (also known as Dr. Nadia). She is a Christian social worker and counselor with over a decade of experience working with all different types of trauma.

Dr. Nadia explained that trauma can interfere with regions of the brain that govern fear and stress responses, emotional regulation, and executive function of the brain. These neurological effects usually increase the risk of developing emotional, behavioral, and mental health issues, especially when the trauma occurs in childhood or is left untreated.

When asked how faith can affect our healing, Dr. Nadia responded unequivocally that faith and professional therapy work hand-in-hand. She believes professional therapy is a great support to our faith. She says recovery among her Christian patients is hands-down more significant and far-reaching than non-Christians.

"When the wounds are deep, you just can't do it alone. God blessed us with doctors, medicine, support groups, and many other resources. When a believer comes to my office, they bring with them the faith that God can heal them, and therapy is the support that helps mend and strengthen their spirit and soul," said Dr. Nadia in our conversation.

You are not reading these words by mistake. The Lover of your soul sees you and desires to save and heal you. Our great, great God divinely placed this book in your hands and He will not leave you busted, broken, and bruised. He longs to make you new and to give you an abundant life full of joy, peace, and love. He wants to transform you and pull you out of that shattered place. If God can work in the lives of those featured on the pages of this devotional book, He will do it for you, too!

Even if some of these stories don't mirror your personal experiences, I invite you to journey with me over the next 60 days as we immerse ourselves in accounts of God's tender care for His children. We will witness addicts finding sobriety, gain insight into the life of a mother who tragically lost her newborn, and read about a God-fearing woman who, despite her own battles with thoughts of suicide, dedicates her life to helping others facing similar struggles. We begin our time together with my story of sexual assault and my very long road to healing.

If you are still easily triggered, I recommend you read this while regularly meeting with a therapist or pastor to help you process your thoughts and emotions.

Every devotional is followed by a day of meditation and prayer. I have written visual and guided reflections for you to read, then practice, in a quiet place with Jesus. I believe it is in these moments alone with our Savior – learning how to communicate with Him and recognize His voice – that we experience the absolute tenderness of God.

Visualizing our Father with us, gazing at us, and wrapping His arms around us is a powerful way to encounter the Lord, who loves you beyond what you can ever imagine. This practice helped me to see God as my gentle and protective Father. I pray these guided moments help you sense God's nearness. If being alone is difficult for you, I encourage you to practice these meditations with a trusted Christian counselor or friend championing your wellness. I have learned that when we create space for intimacy and communion with God, we begin to see Him as a near-to-me-Papa rather than a faraway God who is busy managing the universe.

It is also my prayer that by the time you are done reading this devotional book, you will have *SEEN* the evidence of God's presence in each story and find the courage to begin your pursuit of Jesus and His healing.

Beloved, I hope you know how much God loves you. You are *SEEN* by our Creator! This book is a reminder of that truth. I love you, friend, and oh how I have prayed for you! Now, may the Holy Spirit come upon you as you read, in the mighty name of Jesus.

"The Lord bless you and keep you; the Lord make
his face shine on you and be gracious to you; the
Lord turn his face toward you
and give you peace."
Numbers 6:24-26 NIV

PART ONE

THE BROKENNESS OF SEXUAL VIOLENCE

For those whose hearts and identity have been
shattered by sexual abuse or violence, comfort can
be found in our Father's tender embrace, as He heals
and restores your spirit. Today, He leans toward
your ear and whispers, "I will heal your wounds."
— Jeremiah 30:17 NIV

Day One

Rebecca's Story:
The God Who Sees

The hum of fluorescent lights sang a wicked song over me as I stood naked on a white sheet while nurses poked at my flesh, looking for evidence. The tears fell quietly as my body violently trembled, from my toes up to the tangled and matted mess on my head. The click of the camera capturing scratches and bruising echoed loudly, shaking me from my catatonic state, and then the violent weeping would begin again. The scent of alcohol hung over me like a cloud so thick I nearly wanted to vomit. I wanted to crawl away somewhere to sleep and never wake up again. The white coats around me continued with their rigid collection. I stared into the abyss of dull white walls as they swabbed my mouth, cut some hair, and trimmed my fingernails. On and on it went, for hours, it seemed.

My cries that night came from the deepest part of my soul. I sounded like an off-key tenor singing hell to sleep.

3

The nurses gently tried to comfort me, "Shh, we're almost done, sweetheart, it's going to be ok, shhh."

But I knew in my spirit I would never be the same again. That night, a new label was affixed to my soul. "Rape victim" was my new name. I convinced myself I was far beyond God's reach — too fractured to heal, too dirty for Him to care. Whatever distance I willfully created between me and God was multiplied on that dreadful night.

When violence touches us, we either run from God or run to Him. I chose to run away. It was the beginning of a long, deeply broken, and dysfunctional journey. It was the beginning of going down the rabbit hole of emotional suffering more intense than I could ever comprehend.

Ever been there? What has broken and devastated you to your core? Do you believe God is millions of miles away and too far to reach you? Do you feel invisible in your suffering?

In the Bible, Hagar also felt invisible to God. This servant girl was the victim of an abusive situation that got so toxic she fled to the desert. God knew her pain, and He met her in that dry and lonely desert. Her situation did not miraculously change, but knowing that God saw her and had a future planned for her, changed her.

> *"Thereafter, Hagar used another name to refer to the Lord, who had spoken to her. She said, "You are the God who sees me." - Genesis 16:13 NLT*

Sweet friend, this message is God's way of telling you that He sees you, too. He is gently asking you to surrender "that night, that relationship, loss, or trauma" to the only One who can actually bring meaning to it. Jesus stretched His battered and bloodied arms out on the cross for this moment, and He calls you to Him now.

I know this because I am on the other side of trauma. More than 30 years later, I can see how Father held me on that grim night. But it took nearly two decades before the weight of my shame and depression became too much for me to carry, and I finally surrendered my life to Christ. My Precious Papa put the pieces of my life back together and has given me these words to share with you.

O, how Father loves you! He has hope and healing for you, too! Will you take this step of faith with me?

PRAY WITH ME...

Father, fill me with the strength and courage to say "Yes" to You today. Guide my journey through this book, open my heart, and speak to me. Show me what needs to change in my life, and grant me the courage to step out in faith. Surround me with godly men and women who will love me and speak life into all that feels dead inside of me. May Your Holy Spirit come over me now, in the mighty name of Jesus.

Amen.

Day Two

MEDITATION AND PRAYER: FATHER SEES YOUR SUFFERING

"I can never escape from Your Spirit! I can never get away from your presence! If I go up to heaven, You are there; if I go down to the grave, You are there. If I ride the wings of the morning, if I dwell by the farthest oceans, even there Your hand will guide me, and Your strength will support me. I could ask the darkness to hide me and the light around me to become night — but even in darkness I cannot hide from you."
Psalm 139:7-12 NLT

Our Father's Word reminds us that no matter where we go, we can never take ourselves too far from His reach. Yesterday, we saw that He came for Hagar after she ran off to that lonely desert. Even in that cold and barren place, God was able to reach her. Hagar encountered God and was able to persevere through her difficult circumstances (Genesis 16:13 NLT) because He was with her.

In today's scripture, King David understood that the presence of God inhabited the universe from beginning to end. He paints that picture beautifully for us in Psalm 139. He passionately reminds us that our Father is everywhere, even in the deserts of our lives, and He desires to dwell in you. Your name is on His heart. He sees you right where you are, and He wants to heal and transform your life. You are not invisible to Him. Father is asking you today to let Him in and let Him be your Comforter, your Healer, your Savior.

MEDITATION:

On this day of meditation and prayer, let's reflect on the words of Psalm 139, verses 7-12. Let's go into God's presence and experience His tenderness.

Find a quiet place and get comfortable. Take a deep breath and imagine you are breathing in the sweet presence of God. Exhale all those thoughts and emotions that make you feel invisible. If this is hard for you, that is okay. If you get distracted, that is normal; just acknowledge your wandering and bring your thoughts back into this sacred place.

I like to picture myself sitting on the sand and looking out into the perfection of the ocean. I can see my feet settled in the softness of the sand. As I close my eyes, Father walks up behind me. He sits with me and puts His giant arm of protection around me, then leans over and places a gentle kiss on the top of my head. Try to imagine a place that you love. Maybe it is a room where you feel safe, a garden that helps you escape the day's chaos, or a beach like the one I described. Close your eyes and imagine being in this place with your loving Papa.

Take this tender moment with God to reflect on His holy scripture. Pray the words of the psalm, and invite Father to meet you right where you are. Ask Him to minister to your spirit, then try to stay here for a while.

Pray With Me...

O Gracious, Loving Father,

I can never escape from your Spirit! I can never get away from your presence! If I go up to heaven, you are there; if I go down to the grave, you are there. If I ride the wings of the morning, if I dwell by the farthest oceans, even there, your hand will guide me, and your strength will support me. I could ask the darkness to hide me and the light around me to become night—but even in darkness, I cannot hide from you.

Here I am, Papa. I am Your beloved. Speak to me. I am listening.

Amen.

Day Three

Rebecca's Story: My Mother's Faith and God's Open Hand

My mother, Mercedes, was in the midst of her morning rounds when she heard her name called over the hospital intercom. "Mercedes, you have a call on line three," the operator said. Draped in her well-pressed nurse's scrubs, she headed down the hall and picked up the phone. She did not recognize the voice telling her they needed to discuss an incident that involved me. She quickly told the voice on the line, "I need to take this call in my office. Can you hold on for a minute, please?"

Once behind the safety of her locked door, the voice continued.

"Rebecca is okay, but we need to let you know that she was sexually assaulted a few nights ago. It did not happen on our campus, and she did receive medical attention. She really needs to go home. Mrs. Medina? Are you still there?"

My mom's world began to spin. *This was a lie — not true. It could not be true*, she thought.

She slammed the phone down, picked up her bag, and rushed to get home. Once inside her car, she fell apart and sobbed for a while. When she was able to pull herself back together, she did what she always did when life knocked her down– she prayed and thanked God.

"Lord, she's alive. She'll be okay. She's alive. Thank You, God, for keeping her alive."

Shaken, my mom broke the news to my dad, Pablo, and they grieved for the daughter they knew was gone. They understood even then that the vibrant girl who left home would soon return as a deeply wounded stranger.

When I finally got home, my mom was relieved to find me in one piece, but she says she will never forget the look in my eyes. "Those big brown eyes, once vibrant with life, were hollow and empty — very far away," she said.

"I just could not believe how pale my baby looked underneath her long dark locks, and she still seemed to be in shock – there was this strange silence to her. She was breathing, but there were no signs of life."

Though my mom was glad to have me back home safely, those first few months were torture for her and my dad, especially at night. She would leave the hallway lights on and my bedroom door ajar. I avoided sleep, and she knew it. However, as silence crept over the house, I would eventually drift off to sleep – but only for a little while.

Night after night, my mother would awaken to the harrowing echoes of my reliving the assault. Even now, she recalls those haunting sounds "ripping her soul apart." Each sleepless night, she would swiftly transition into mom-mode, rushing down the hall to cradle me in her arms, gently coaxing me from the clutches of the nightmare that ensnared me.

"Shh, you are okay. You are safe. Shh. It's okay, baby. I got you, you're okay," she uttered over and over as she rocked me back to sleep.

Some nights, my dad would stand in the hallway pacing nervously, feeling helpless, and unsure of what to do for me. My mom trusted God with every ounce of her soul, but she often wondered if she would ever see her child smile again – thrive again.

Friend, do you have someone in your life who can't escape their nightmares? Do you wonder if God will ever restore them?

My fearless mother often prayed, "Father, my heart cries! Only You can heal my daughter and make her whole. Protect her mind, God, and her spirit. She is Yours, You gave her to me – I trust You to restore her, Father, and complete Your promise to me."

Months turned into years and years into decades before my recovery came. The path was not a straight line either! It was a bumpy road with many setbacks. But my faithful mama kept believing and trusting in the God who saved her long ago. She often thanked Him for a healing that had not come yet. She spent a lot of time in the Bible and prayed the scriptures over my life and my scars. She especially held onto James 5:16.

"Confess your trespasses to one another, and pray for one another, that you may be healed. The effective, fervent prayer of a righteous man avails much." James 5:16 NKJV

Refusing to accept her daughter's brokenness as permanent, she persisted in prayer. It often seemed as if nothing was happening, and I was being swallowed up by the black cloud of depression. But my mother did finally see God answer her prayers. Nearly two decades after that harrowing night, I surrendered my life, my shame, and my trauma to Jesus. My mother has seen God's goodness, and she shares this message with you today:

"Never stop praying, never stop trusting God – especially when it seems nothing is happening. He is faithful!" Mercedes said.

Friend, this warrior-mom's fervent, expectant prayers activated our Heavenly Father's power in beautiful ways. Jesus repaired what was broken in my life, and He healed the deep wounds that our family carried.

Will you lift your head toward heaven and choose to trust that God will open His healing hand for the one you love?

PRAY WITH ME...

Blessed Father,

You are a giant to Your children! Help us to remember You this way when we approach Your throne weary, afraid, and brokenhearted. Lord, may we grab ahold of your open hand. Thank You, Papa, for praying mothers and fathers. Meet them where they are - comfort their hearts, take away their doubts, and heal their children. In the name of Jesus.

Amen.

Day Four

MEDITATION AND PRAYER: FATHER SEES YOUR NEED FOR COMFORT

"All praise to God, the Father of our Lord Jesus Christ. God is our merciful Father and the source of all comfort. He comforts us in all our troubles so that we can comfort others. When they are troubled, we will be able to give them the same comfort God has given us."
2 Corinthians 1:3-4 NLT

When my mother, Mercedes, chose to surrender her burdened heart and profound suffering to Jesus, her cares and concerns did not magically go away. Healing for my family took a long time. My mom always trusted God had a plan and He would repurpose our family's pain somehow. It was not easy, but she remained confident that He would use this tragic event that changed our lives to comfort others one day. She knew it would happen because she trusts God is who He says He is!

When the circumstances before Mercedes' human eyes made her doubt the goodness of God, prayer steered her focus back to her Great Comforter. When the haunting despair in my eyes was too much for her, she would go to her quiet place with God, fall to her knees, and pray. Jesus reassured her spirit every time.

Mercedes said she would hear Him whisper deep into her spirit, "I will always keep My promises to you, daughter."

I absolutely believe Jesus leaned in and bent His ear toward Mercedes every time He heard her cry out in pain. When she doubted, she prayed. When she was frustrated, she prayed. When she felt like giving up, she prayed some more. My mumsy wants you to know that God adores you and your children. You are His pride and joy! He will answer your prayers and comfort you in your time of need. Then, one day, it will be your turn to embrace another suffering similar pain and remind them that our Father is listening, watching, and working, even when it does not seem like it.

Thanks be to God, our Strong and Mighty Fortress!

MEDITATION:

On this day of meditation and prayer, let's reflect on the words of 2 Corinthians. Let's enter our tranquil sanctuary with God, where we can experience His comforting presence.

Have you settled into a quiet place? Begin to breathe slowly and deeply.

Begin to visualize yourself in a crowded department store. With a frantic sense of urgency, you stop shoppers and ask if they have seen your child. "How could I lose them? How?" you think. You hear your child's name blared over the store's intercom system, and you begin to feel sick to your stomach. Your heart beats faster and faster. You close your eyes and begin to pray. Suddenly, you realize you are not alone. A soft and gentle breeze passes through your body.

God is with you.

You open your eyes, and God is standing before you with your beloved child in His arms. God looks at you, lovingly. You cannot break your eyes away from His powerful gaze, and He says, "I gave this child to you, but I've never let them go. Trust Me with our baby."

Pray With Me...

Father,

You are a giant in my eyes, and I entrust my child's safety and healing into Your loving hands. I praise and worship You, God of all comfort. I trust You will make my child whole again so they may comfort other hurting children and testify of the goodness of God.

May Your divine protection surround them. Holy Spirit, I call on Your power and authority to bind the forces of darkness that seek to hurt my child. Lord, may Your presence work like healing balm in my child's spirit. In Jesus' name, I pray.

Amen.

Day Five

REBECCA'S STORY: GOD, WHERE WERE YOU?

Four years after the assault, I finally returned to school and completed my degree in Mass Communications, embarking on a career as a television journalist. As my busy career in news flourished, I found myself frequently relocating to new cities with each new contract. Yet, despite the excitement of new opportunities, the stench of my past always followed.

After a decade of covering local government and crime, I found myself overwhelmed by bitterness and emotional turmoil. I was tired and longed for something I could not articulate. It had been twenty years since the assault, and I was living in Tampa, grappling with profound sadness and depression. Seeking solace, I began quietly attending church on Sunday mornings, wrestling with the haunting question, "Where were You, God, when I was hurt?"

As the worship team belted out songs of praise, I struggled to reconcile my belief in a God who seemed absent in my darkest hour. But even in my anger and confusion, I continued to show up, and little by little, the Father's Word penetrated the concrete walls I erected around my damaged heart. I felt vulnerable as if the dam built around my spirit was preparing to collapse. As I wrestled with the memories of that night, I continued to shake my fists at God. On the other hand, my patient Father was dealing with my heart.

I started dreaming of a faint light under the door of the room where I was confined on that pivotal night. When the weight of my attacker was too much and I could no longer wrestle him off, when the fight inside me was no more, I locked my eyes on that light. Somehow, that dim glow took me far away and helped me survive those moments.

My search for answers led me to the Bible, and I came across John 11:33-35 NLT.

When Jesus saw her weeping and saw the other people wailing with her, a deep anger welled up within Him, and He was deeply troubled. "Where have you put him?" He asked them.
They told Him, "Lord, come and see."
Then Jesus wept.

This scripture highlights the humanity of Jesus. Though He knew He would resurrect Lazarus, Jesus was profoundly moved by Mary and Martha's anguish. They were Lazarus' sisters, and the Bible says, "Jesus wept" when He saw their grief. These verses offer immense comfort and affirm if the God of the Universe is moved to tears by the suffering of His friends, surely He shares in our pain. It speaks to a significant truth: if He wept for them, He surely weeps with us when we face life's traumas.

We live in a world that is dark and evil. Bad things will happen to us at some point in our lives, but Jesus never leaves us. He weeps with us, then strengthens us for the road ahead. I recognize today that the light which held my gaze decades ago became my refuge in a moment of terror and confusion. I still dream about that light. That light was my Blessed Father, and The radiance of His glory overtook the darkness in my life.

Dear friend, Jesus wants you to know He was there with you in your despair, and He wept. Some might suggest God ordains terrible things to happen so you can learn and grow from them. I disagree. This would suggest that Jesus is a cruel teacher willing to abuse us so that we draw near to Him. He never gave Lazarus' family that speech — He felt their pain, cried with them, and does the same with you!

I still carry deep sadness for my 18-year-old self, but I also hold onto the hope of God's ongoing healing, acknowledging that it's a lifelong journey. It's okay to feel sorrow for the traumatic events in our lives while remaining expectant of God's goodness. One can survive trauma without God, but I believe our chances of thriving past the battering blows of life are much more possible and sustaining through the work and power of the Holy Spirit.

If you wrestle with the question of "why" something happened to you, take it to our Blessed Father. He is big, powerful, and secure enough to handle our "why" questions. I caution you, however, be prepared to learn amazing things about God's love, grace, and mercy.

Pray With Me...

Blessed Father,

I trust that You are kind, compassionate, and passionately in love with Your children. I believe that You feel the hurt and agony we experience during tragic events in our lives. I accept that on this side of eternity, we may never understand why some things happen. Lord, I pray for You to speak to my heart when I struggle with the 'whys' of my life. Help me to deal with my scars and surrender them to You. We declare Your promise of healing over everyone reading these words today. Holy Spirit, renew and refresh us now, in the name of Jesus.

Amen.

Day Six

Meditation and Prayer: Father Sees The Confusion You Struggle With

"So do not fear, for I am with you; do not be dismayed, for I am your God. I will strengthen you and help you; I will uphold you with my righteous right hand."
Isaiah 41:10 NIV

Isaiah is considered one of the greatest prophets ever to live. He prophesied the birth, death, and resurrection of Jesus Christ. Though the book of Isaiah is steeped in some of the deepest theological truths, it is also packed with prophetic promises for you and me and everything we would ever face on this side of heaven.

In Isaiah 41:10, His word assures us that we do not have to be afraid or discouraged because we serve a God who is with us and for us! Isaiah never says that God will keep us from experiencing bad things. He does not say that the sin of the world will never touch us. Instead, he assures us that God will strengthen and sustain us through the tragedies of our lives.

Beloved, this word is for you! Don't drown in your questions and confusion — take it all to the One who can handle all things. God is infinite and supreme. Because He is sovereign, Jesus does not have to explain anything to us. Yet, He still allows us to take our "whys" to Him. That blows my mind!

You are the apple of God's eye, created in His image, and our compassionate King desires to deal with the confusion you may struggle with over why something occurred in your life. Jesus invites you to bring it all to Him.

MEDITATION:

On this day of meditation and prayer, let's reflect on Isaiah 41:10. May the words of this Old Testament promise fill the broken parts of your heart with God's tenderness. May you be drawn to Him.

Find a quiet place and get comfortable. You may not see Him, but He is there with you. Take a deep breath and inhale the sweet aroma of His presence. Exhale blame, indignation, and anything distracting you from this moment of stillness with your Father. If your mind begins to wander, that is normal. Gently bring your thoughts back into this holy and sacred place.

Picture yourself sitting alone under a tree overlooking a field of golden sunflowers. As the winds shift and brush the side of your face, you catch the delicate scent of these impressive flowers. The nutty and mild aromatherapy instantly put you at ease. As you close your eyes to take it all in, you suddenly realize the presence beside you. Jesus is sitting with you. He puts His hand on your shoulder, leans in, and whispers the words of Isaiah.

"Do not fear, child. Here I AM. Do not be dismayed, for I AM your God. I AM strengthening you and helping you. I AM holding you up with My very hand. Do you trust Me, child?"

Pray With Me...

Compassionate King,

Forgive us for shaking our fists at You. We are so grateful that You are more than just sovereign — You are kind and understanding. Father, I surrender my questions to You.

"Where were You? Why did You leave me? Why did this happen to me? Will I ever be happy again?"

Lord, I wait on Your answers. Address the heaviness in my heart. Fill me with peace and understanding. Strengthen me and uphold me. Help me to recognize the work You are doing in my life. Lord, not my will, but Your will be done.

Amen.

Day Seven

REBECCA'S STORY: THE YOKE OF SHAME

The man who sexually assaulted me was prosecuted and spent some time behind bars. But the entire experience left me deeply wounded. Like the scorching symbol on a sturdy steer's hide, the words "victim, cheap, dirty, and worthless" were burned into my soul.

Life was already very dark, but by the time I left the courthouse, I was spiritually dead, and I was sinking in the quicksand of shame. I felt so filthy I often avoided making eye contact with myself in the mirror. It was discomforting to see anyone peering at me, even if it was myself. I was disgusted with myself and afraid that everyone could see it.

Years of night terrors left me sleepless. My work in TV News was a great distraction, so I put in long hours, nights, and weekends to forget my past. I continued to make destructive choices and entertained bad relationships. To the world, I looked successful and put together, which quieted the shame that weighed on me like the fractured Titanic headed for the abyss of darkness and death. When I did manage to fall asleep, I dreamt of evil standing at the foot of my bed in a long black coat, watching and waiting to torment me. I dreamt of the man who hurt me.

Dear friend, are you lost in shame and guilt like I was? Do you believe what happened to you is who you are? In the name of Jesus, be free from that lie! Let's take a look at what His Word tells us.

> *"I sought the Lord, and He answered me; He delivered me from all my fears. Those who look to Him are radiant; their faces are never covered in shame." Psalm 34:4-5 NIV*

On the day that you were hurt, violated, or betrayed, our common enemy, Satan, dispatched His army of fallen angels to destroy your peace and purpose. He wants you stuck in this place because he knows once your chains break, so will the yoke he placed over you on that dark day.

You are not responsible for what happened to you, dear friend. God wants you to know you are not cheap, dirty, or worthless. You are HIS HOLY CREATION, and He wiped the canvas of your life clean when you confessed that He was your Savior. You are perfect in His eyes, and He wants to wash away the stain of your trauma and heal the brokenness left behind. You were never meant to carry this cross. Your Savior, Jesus Christ, already carried it for you.

Beloved, when we hold onto shame and guilt, we tell Father that the sacrifice of His Only Son was not enough! Receive His gift of healing and wholeness, then do the work. Find yourself a Christian counselor and a church community to pray with and encourage you. Finally, pick up your Bible. You must combat the enemy's lies with God's truth.

This is a lifelong process, but the days become brighter, the pain lessens, and healing happens, thanks be to God. My life today is evidence of His goodness, and I know He loves you every bit as much as He loves me.

PRAY WITH ME...

Holy God,

Help me to sense Your presence as I pray these words. I surrender my guilt and shame to You now. Lord, I thank You for removing the yoke of shame from me today. Surround me with godly people who will help me. Give me the courage to face my past so I can be whole again. I receive Your healing today. I receive Your freedom. I trust Your will and Your way for me. Holy Spirit, begin Your work in me now.

Amen.

Day Eight

MEDITATION AND PRAYER: FATHER SEES THE CONFUSION YOU STRUGGLE WITH

"There is therefore now no condemnation for those who are in Christ Jesus."
Romans 8:1 ESV

Shame is a common response for victims of sexual violence or abuse. Though individual experiences may vary, the shame many of us feel after the assault can be intense and overwhelming, especially if those feelings are internalized or go untreated. Friend, the shame you may feel is part of the trauma left behind by the evil committed against you.

You must believe that you are not responsible for what happened to you. The blame falls solely on your perpetrator. It does not matter what you were wearing, if you were intoxicated, where you were, or who you were with. Your body is a gift from God, and when that criminal violated you, they sinned against you and your Father. I shudder at the thought of that person going before The Judge of All Creation one day to account for the crimes committed against you and me.

You still have breath in your lungs, which means healing is possible, restoration is promised, and joy is coming.

Romans 8:1 promises the children of God that we stand before Him with zero disapproval. Friend, if you have a relationship with God, this scripture in Romans means we are not condemned for the sins of our past, the sins committed against us, and the sins we will commit in the future.

Father's compassion for you is boundless, and He loves you so much He left you a love letter — the Bible, to assure you: *"There is therefore NO condemnation for those who are in Christ Jesus."*

Jesus died in a disgraceful way – naked and exposed. He suffered the utmost shame so that you would be free from it. Jesus paid the price for the day when you would come into His presence ashamed and afraid, only to hear Papa say to you, "I was with you, child. I saw it all, and it was not your fault. Leave your shame, guilt, and humiliation with Me now, and let Me restore your life."

MEDITATION:

On this day of meditation and prayer, let's reflect on the words of Romans 8:1. Together, let's immerse ourselves in the presence of the Almighty and bask in His tenderness.

Make sure you are somewhere quiet and where you cannot be interrupted. Take a few deep breaths and simply let yourself be embraced by the stillness and silence around you. Imagine that as you sit in the quiet, The Judge of All Creation enters the room. His presence is blinding as He walks toward you. His love is everywhere, and you begin to look up as He gently takes your hand in His. You catch a glimpse of the scars on His mighty hands; the Son of God is with you! He explains that His scars should remind you He sacrificed His very life so you would be healed. He was humiliated and shamed on the cross so you would be free of it all.

Stay here for a bit. When you are ready, pray the words of Romans 8:1 and invite Him to work in you now.

PRAY WITH ME...

Blessed Jesus,

You suffered so I would not carry this self-blame and shame. You were whipped, and Your body was broken for me. I declare today that what You promised long ago is the truth, and I am not condemned because I am in a relationship with You. I profess this truth over my life, in the name of Jesus. I receive Your restoration now. Thank You for Your immeasurable love and patience. Help me to sense your tenderness now. I love You, Father.

Amen.

Day Nine

REBECCA'S STORY: RESTORED TRUST

I grew up in a legalistic church that taught me more about the wrath and punishment of God than His grace and mercy. The length of someone's skirt or a congregant's deep shade of lipstick was enough to garner stares harder than the wooden pews lining both sides of the giant sanctuary. The first time I ever felt shamed was by my pastor for wearing a pair of shorts in the summer — I was nine years old.

For a long time, I believed that God was only interested in condemning me. As a child, I often pictured Him as a scary figure with an angry scowl, watching and waiting for me to sin. Once I was old enough, I ran from the church and vowed never to return. My young adult life became one sinful act after another. By the time I was sexually assaulted (in 1992), God was nothing more than a dark and distant childhood memory. But even in my denial of Jesus, I still feared Him in an unhealthy way. I believed that rape, sadness, and despair were God's punishment for the way I lived my life.

I told myself things like, "I should never have been there. I deserved it. My choices led to that horrible night. I'm dirty and used up."

But our God is so loving and compassionate. Even in those haunting moments, I would hear a faint whisper in the deepest part of my soul reminding me, "You said no."

I believe God was trying to reach me, even though I rejected Him. Friends, I had a trust problem with our Creator. I wanted to believe He was a good father, but an unhealthy picture of God kept me in my dysfunction.

Sunday morning services were helping me cope, but it was a midweek prayer service that changed everything. I was reintroduced to a kind and compassionate God, a Father who did not send His Only Son to die on the cross to condemn me but to save me (John 3:17 NIV).

As I delved into the Bible for the first time, everything I learned about God shattered the wall of lies I had come to believe. I encountered the story of Mary Magdalene, a broken woman afflicted by demonic oppression. Jesus healed her, and she went on to become an important part of His earthly ministry. Similarly, the Samaritan woman, despite her past, found redemption in the loving embrace of our Savior at the well. These narratives revealed to me that God isn't concerned with my perfection but with my sincere devotion and repentance. However, it was the story of the woman with the issue of blood that lit the match to my healing.

This woman suffered from a debilitating illness that caused her to bleed for twelve years. Her medical condition meant she was considered ceremonially unclean by society and, therefore, could not be around other people, even family. Nor was she allowed to participate in religious activities. Can you imagine the loneliness she felt?

When Jesus came to town, crowds gathered around Him. Recognizing this as her only chance for healing, she thought, *"If I just touched His clothes, I will be healed"* (Mark 5:28 NIV). But her condition and pressure of the crowd made close contact impossible. In her desperation, she pressed her way through the crowd anyway. Just as Jesus seemed out of reach, she fell to the ground, and the hem of His garment slid through her fingers.

> *Jesus said, "Someone deliberately touched me, for I felt healing power go out from me." When the woman realized that she could not stay hidden, she began to tremble and fell to her knees in front of him. The whole crowd heard her explain why she had touched him and that she had been immediately healed. "Daughter," he said to her, "your faith has made you well. Go in peace."*
> *Luke 8:46-48 NIV*

The loving way that Jesus addressed the woman helped me understand His true character. He called her "daughter." She is the only woman in all the Bible whom He refers to as "daughter." He stopped everything to find her. She may have been unclean and invisible to her community, but Jesus never saw her that way. I understood for the first time my Heavenly Father is nothing like what I grew up believing. I could trust Him with anything, including my healing.

Friends, in some ways, we are all like the woman with the issue of blood, and Father desires to make us whole again. He wants us to trust Him with our sin, dysfunction, diagnosis, and everything else that plagues us. But, like this woman, we must step out in faith and push past the obstacles and through the crowd to experience transformation. Beloved, come alongside me, grab hold of my hand, and together, let's reach for The Healer's holy garment.

Pray With Me...

LORD,

I am not sure that I believe You can heal me and transform my life. Help me with my unbelief. Give me the courage and strength to shift my focus from my obstacles to endless possibilities because of who You are – my Healer and Redeemer. Lord, thank You for kicking down the lies the world has fed me, and for showing me who You are and what You desire for Your children. Holy Spirit, rest on me now and make me new.

Amen

Day Ten

MEDITATION AND PRAYER: FATHER SEES YOUR STRUGGLE TO TRUST AGAIN

"Those who know Your name, trust in You, for You, O LORD, do not abandon those who search for You." Psalm 9:10 NLT

How do you perceive God, His Son, and the Holy Spirit? Let's give that question some real thought. Do you believe in your heart that God is all-powerful, that He is good, and that He wants what is best for you?

I love that the Psalms cover just about every bad thing that could happen to us on this side of eternity. King David, who is known as "the man after God's own heart," experienced many highs in his life, but if you read about him, you will quickly see that he lived through many more lows. David was betrayed, lived as a fugitive for a time, dealt with a lot of family drama and dysfunction, committed crimes, experienced the death of a couple of his children, and some scholars believe he likely suffered from depression. Yet, no matter how dark things became, though he may have doubted God, David never stopped trusting Him.

David had a personal relationship with God and spent a lot of time with Him in worship and prayer. He also experienced the faithfulness of God throughout his life. But even David wrestled with feeling like God had abandoned him. He often asked God why his enemies were winning and would cry out to Him in great despair and anguish. But almost as soon as he did these things, he would turn back to God and worship Him. This great king always came back to what he knew for sure – no matter how bad his circumstances were, God is eternal and sovereign, and therefore, He is in control. David reminded himself of all that God had brought him through and came to the conclusion that God was a King of His word and would always keep His covenant with David.

In Psalm 9, David praises God for coming through for him – showing him once again that the King is truly faithful to those who seek Him. The promise in verse 10 is all about security. If you make God your refuge, you will find your safe place. If you dwell in Father's presence, you will discover your residence in His heart – and His in yours. Sweet friend, you cannot be abandoned by the One whose Spirit lives in you and promises to be with you until the end of the age (Matthew 28:20 NLT).

We often hold God to our human standards. When He does not respond or interact with us in our human way, we assume He's left us. The King of kings is omnipotent and too great for us to fully understand. That is part of the mystery of God. But make no mistake, the moment you trust Him as your personal Lord and Savior, the covenant is sealed with the blood He spilled on the cross. He does not abandon those who know His name – Thanks be to God!

David's perception of our Savior was the result of His clinging to Him. As we draw near to the Father, He reveals Himself to us in intimate and tender ways, addressing the pains of our souls and the circumstances of our lives. Our perception of God is formed by our time spent with Him or the lack thereof. We cannot truly know and experience His faithfulness from a distance.

MEDITATION:

On this day of meditation and prayer, let's reflect on the words of Psalm 9:10. It's time to enter God's sanctuary to be enveloped by His kindness and compassion.

Go into your quiet place. Take a few deep breaths, and imagine that you are inhaling the sweet presence of God. Exhale lack of trust. Let go of unbelief. If distractions come your way, acknowledge them and gently bring your thoughts back into this blessed place.

Picture yourself sitting on a park bench surrounded by lush gardens and giant oaks that shade you from the afternoon sun. The light is radiant over you, and there is a breeze that cools your skin. You catch the fragrance of the red and white tulips slowly dancing in the wind when you hear the soft footsteps of Jesus coming toward you. His presence is inviting, and you feel the Lord drawing you to Him. He sits beside you on the bench; you look down and set your eyes on His white robe. The fabric is made of soft silk, something finer and more satiny than you have ever seen. You feel Him put His arm around you, and He tenderly pulls you closer. You have never felt love like this before. It overwhelms you to your core. You lay your head on Him, and He asks you to share all the reasons why you struggle to trust Him. Papa is here, and He wants you to confide in Him.

As we pray the words of Psalm 9:10, let's reflect on the perfection of our Father. His character is trustworthy and good. King Jesus cannot lie, nor will He ever let you down or leave you.

Pray With Me...

O Father,

You are my Lord and Savior. Help me now to trust You with my life and my healing. I depend on You to treat my trauma and restore my life. I believe You are a loving and generous God who will never leave me and wants what is best for me. I know Your name, Father, and I believe You know mine. I will seek You all the days of my life in hopeful anticipation of experiencing Your glory here on earth, as it is in heaven. It is in Your name, Jesus, that I pray these things.

Amen

Day Eleven

CHITO'S STORY: THE DREAM THAT BROUGHT HER HOME

At five years old, Chito was a spunky and fearless little girl with big eyes the color of chestnuts – pudgy cheeks and a vibrant smile. She spent her days running and playing in the tiny Nigerian town where she grew up. It was a warm place where everyone knew each other, and neighbors were like trusted family. That was especially important for her family since her father had left when she was just a little girl.

On one particular day, Chito went next door to a neighbor's house to play, as she often did with the other children. The smell of traditional Nigerian flavors permeated the air with its savory aroma as she curiously skipped through the house. She noticed a closed door down the hall, and without hesitation, she made her way across the vinyl flooring, noticing each of the tiles was a different shade of chocolate. She opened the door and found the neighbor's 16-year-old son sitting in the room watching TV. The room had a large, brown couch that sat over an even bigger area rug of the same color. It all looked so big against the humble cream-colored walls. Chito was instantly drawn to the television — there was no funny cartoon or happy game show playing on the screen. Instead, she observed grown-ups doing things to children about her age that she had never seen before, and the door slowly closed behind her.

That was the first time Chito was abused and groomed into performing sexual favors for the neighbor's son. The sexual abuse went on for 12 years. By the time Chito was 17, she had been molested, abused, and raped by different men and women, all of whom were known to her family. Everything she grew to know and understand about relationships and intimacy was distorted and confused. Watching pornography became a norm for her, as did same-sex relationships or dating men much too old for her. By the time she was in her 20s, she was convinced there was something profoundly wrong with her. She believed the lie that she was rotten to her core.

Despite being in her twenties, Chito carried the weight of a lifetime on her weary shoulders. Abuse had stolen her youthful vibrancy, but a flicker of defiance remained. With a secret hope for change, she relocated to the U.S. to study, embarking on a journey across continents in search of a new beginning. But dysfunction followed, and she was haunted by her childhood.

In 2015, exhausted by her promiscuous lifestyle, she began to seek out a relationship with God. Chito came from a religious family — the church was a community her mother relied on, but it had been a long time since she looked for God.

She sought Jesus in prayer, and in her conversations with Him, she would often ask, "Can I really be pure?" The idea seemed ridiculous to her. She could not believe that God could redeem her life and make her new, so she returned to her destructive dating patterns, sex, and pornography. By 2021, she was secretly engaged to marry a woman in the U.S. But days before that wedding was to take place, she received a call from home with a prophetic message from her grandfather's pastor, whom she had never met.

This Nigerian pastor had a dream that Chito was standing near an ocean, ready to board a boat. The pastor said if she got on the boat, she would never make it to her destination, and God's plan for her life would not come to pass. It was the first time that she ever felt seen and loved by God. Shocked by the revelation of this message, she prayed, "You see me. Lord, You see me. Help me." The words of Psalm 33:13-15 came to life in her spirit that day, and she knew that Father was with her.

"The Lord looks down from heaven and sees the whole human race. From His throne, He observes all who live on the earth. He made their hearts, so He understands everything they do."
Psalm 33:13-15 NLT

She ended her relationship and sought out a church in her new home in South Florida. She threw herself into the Word of God, determined to change her life. During her time spent in prayer and reading her Bible, the Lord gently revealed to her that she had been acting out from her abusive experiences from her childhood. As He comforted her, He also revealed that many of her choices stemmed from the crimes committed against her, but it was not who she was and that one day, she would console others with similar stories.

Chito has fervently sought the Lord, and He has tenderly helped her navigate her journey toward healing. She knows her road to recovery will be a long and arduous one, but she is confident that with God, she will be healed from the scars of her abuse.

When this interview was penned, Chito was getting ready to begin Christian counseling. She is happily practicing celibacy. She says her relationship with God is the first healthy relationship she has ever had, and she fully trusts that He holds her life and future in His hands.

PRAY WITH ME...

Father,

You see everything that happens to us, how we respond, and how we suffer. I know You are not responsible for what happened to me — I know that I live in a broken world where evil resides. But this darkness has caused me so much confusion and dysfunction, and I am asking You now to turn it all around for Your glory. I am confident that my story is not over until You say so! You have the power to heal me, transform everything about my life, and restore all that has been stolen from me. Begin Your work in me — I need You, Jesus. Protect me and lead me to the right resources. God, I ask You now to let me sense Your presence here with me. It is in Your name that I pray.

Amen.

Day Twelve

MEDITATION AND PRAYER: FATHER SEES YOUR STRUGGLE TO FORGIVE YOURSELF

*"Therefore, if anyone is in Christ, the new creation
has come: The old has gone, the new is here!"*
2 Corinthians 5:17 NIV

The enemy works diligently to deploy one of his greatest deceptions: convincing victims of sexual abuse and violence that they somehow asked for it or deserved it due to something they did. Sex itself becomes distorted in the mind of the abused, and with that, the truth about the very act that was given to humanity as a gift to be received and enjoyed in the covenant of marriage.

Father desires to place His corrective lens over your eyes today. He aims to refresh your perspective, remind you of the truth about what happened to you, and He hopes, as I do, that you will grab hold of the promise in today's scripture and make it your own.

He's watched you replay images of the tragic events over and over again in your head, almost as if you could go back and change everything. Beloved, it's tiring, hopeless, and works like a quickly-spreading infection of the soul.

If you were sexually abused as a child, I want to remind you — you were never expected to protect yourself or think like an adult. Abusers are insidious and cunning in how they target the vulnerable. They employ tricks and bribes that children, in their innocence, are ill-equipped to navigate.

If you were an adult who was violated, know that God abhors what transpired. Whether it was a violent attack or coercion against your will, it should never have occurred. It was unjust and deeply sorrowful.

God is the Master of making us new! When we were saved, we were born again. All of our sins were forgiven, and our lives were washed clean. The enemy uses abuse to try to make us believe we are guilty and will never be clean or whole again. He tries to taint or tarnish God's agenda for our lives. Do not buy the lies the enemy is trying to sell you!

Here are four truths to meditate on and practice as you begin the process of taking back your life!

1. Tell yourself over and over again, "The abuse perpetrated against me was not my fault. What

happened to me was a crime, and I am in no way guilty." Any guilt or self-blame is a false narrative. Write these statements down, add some reassuring scripture (like Romans 8:33, Proverbs 3:5-6, and Isaiah 41:10), keep it where you can see it, and repeat it to yourself. Your feelings and emotions will catch up!

2. Surrender everything you feel and have believed over the years to God. Invite Him to heal the painful memories. Ask Him to hush the accuser's voice. Choose today to let go of navigating your pain your way and let Jesus into the driver's seat of your life. Choose to trust what He says, *"Child, if you are in Me, you are a new creation: The old you is gone, the new is here!"* Write your name into this verse and keep it where you can see it on a regular basis.

3. Refuse to let the enemy use what happened to you to keep you from God's plans for your life. If you are consumed by self-hatred, unforgiveness, and resentment for yourself or your abuser, you distance yourself from God. Work with a trusted Christian counselor to walk you through these deep caverns of pain embedded in your soul. God saved you, and your life is filled with unimaginable purpose. Ask Him to lead you to a place of love, grace, and mercy so that you can be healed.

4. Remember, you are not alone! There are many men and women who struggle with similar trauma. But once you claim God's truth, that He can

wash away any painful stain, He begins to empower and equip you to help others who have suffered in the same ways. This in and of itself can become a powerful source of continued healing for anyone stuck in the darkness of Satan's lies.

Friend, although you will always carry the memories of what happened to you, know that you can find freedom from the damage your perpetrators intended to inflict upon you.

MEDITATION:

On this day of meditation and prayer, let's reflect on the words of 2 Corinthians 5:17. Let's journey into the arms of the Creator, where His tenderness awaits us.

Take a deep breath, shut out the distractions, and imagine that you are breathing in the healing presence of God. Exhale all hopelessness. If the enemy tries to tell you this is useless, rebuke that lie in The name of Jesus.

Picture yourself alone, sitting before a sprawling playground. The vibrant colors of the seesaw, swings, and sandbox overwhelm you with sadness. As you sit on the grass, you begin to mourn your childhood. You weep over your lost innocence, the shame you've carried, and the torment of guilt. A mighty wind forces you to shut your eyes. You cannot explain it, but instantly, you realize Jesus is in the wind. You don't understand it, but it is so. He's here with you – all around you. As you slowly open your eyes, He takes your hand, and you see the scars from where the nails once were. Like a curious child, you trace the mark on His hand with your index finger.

"You see that, child?" says the Lord.

"I know what it's like to suffer too. I understand your pain and confusion. Let Me take it from you now – you have carried it all for far too long. I made you a new creation long ago, do you believe Me? My wounds have covered your pain, child. I sacrificed everything just for you – do you want to be healed?"

PRAY WITH ME...

Father,

I give You my life, my childhood trauma, my fears, difficult memories, and anxieties. You promise that if I am Yours, I am "a new creation; the old is gone, and the new is here." I receive Your promise and declare it over my life. Lord, give me the strength to believe this, the boldness to tell my story, and the discernment to know when the enemy is attempting to confuse me. Satan's torment ends today – right now! Take this burden from me and pour Your healing balm into my spirit. In the mighty name of Jesus.

Amen.

PART TWO

THE BROKENNESS
OF GRIEF

In the deepest throes of anguish and sorrow, God
will gently heal the brokenness of grief. You will
never be the same, but He promises to carry you
through the valleys of death and darkness. All the
while He whispers, "I AM with you."
(Psalm 23:4 CSB)

Day Thirteen

MARIA'S STORY: JONAH'S MOM

It was Christmas Day 2013 when Maria and Isaac walked hand-in-hand into the hospital. Maria was 34 weeks pregnant with Jonah Ilan Rosado, and an unusual pain made her pack up and go to the hospital, thinking her third son was destined to be a Christmas baby. "How fitting," Maria thought. She had waited so long for this child.

But Maria would leave the hospital days later without their son and in unimaginable mental and emotional anguish.

Jonah was strangled by his own umbilical cord, and shortly after the devastating news, he was taken from Maria's womb by cesarean. When Maria awoke from surgery, there he was in his bassinet. Perfectly pink, warm to the touch, and his dark baby hair poked out from underneath his hospital hat. He was perfect, and she was convinced it was all a mistake.

Still tethered to an IV and woozy from anesthesia, Maria held Jonah and anointed him with her tears. She pressed her face to his, trying to freeze this final moment in her memory. She inhaled the smell of her newborn, ran her nose over his soft cheeks, and said goodbye.

Maria was a pastor's wife who followed God her whole life. Surely, her loving Father would never let this happen to her precious child, "or would He?" she thought. She felt confused and responsible, as if she brought all this grief upon her husband and family on her own. She felt as though she failed, her body failed, and all she wanted was to die with her baby boy.

Dear friend, were you forced to bury your hopes and dreams with your baby? Are you deep in sorrow and unable to shake the ache of empty arms? Are you angry at God?

Months after the loss of her precious boy, Maria limped through Christian counseling. She struggled with severe PTSD and was trying her best to move on with her family. In the quiet moments, however, her memories would transport her back to that hospital room, and the grief would rush over her again and again. One particular Sunday morning, a prophetic minister visited her church, and when he saw her, he shared a special word with her.

"What happened to you was not God's fault," he said. "It was a tragic accident, and in your moment of mourning, He mourned with you and carried you through, Maria."

Standing before this pastor, she realized her Tender Papa saw her, and He was working in her pain. In the months that followed Jonah's death, God perfectly placed women in Maria's path who suffered their own losses. She was able to connect with these mothers in ways no one else could. Maria was reminded of the words of Jeremiah.

"I chose you before I formed you in the womb; I set you apart before you were born. I appointed you a prophet to the nations."
Jeremiah 1:5 CSB

She slowly began to understand that her Heavenly Father loved Jonah more than she ever could. God knew Jonah before he was even conceived; he belonged to God before he belonged to her. Though his life was short, it was filled with purpose. His life is her ministry! God entrusted Maria with this pain to reach you. Perhaps you are still reeling from the loss of someone you deeply love. Dear friend, what happened was tragic, but it was not God's fault, nor is it your fault.

Father wants you to know He has been holding you, and He wants to mend your broken heart. Your spirit will always bear the scar of loss on this side of eternity, but our loving God guarantees you will see the one you love, alive and well, on the other side. Maria lives with that hope and says she knows exactly what she will say when she sees Jonah again.

"Oh, how I've missed you!"

Pray With Me...

Father,

Forgive me for my anger. I sense You trying to reach me in the midst of this darkness. I do not know the way out, but I trust that You do. I trust You will help me and work on my broken spirit. I believe that, even in my pain, You are good – I just don't feel that right now. My pain reaches to the core of my existence, and some days, I feel like life will swallow me up. Help me, Papa. I place my heart in Your hands. May Your peace wash over me. In the name of Jesus.

Amen.

Day Fourteen

MEDITATION AND PRAYER: FATHER SEES YOUR LOSS

*"Blessed are those who mourn, for they
will be comforted."*
Matthew 5:4 CSB

Matthew 5:4 is one of the first verses in the Beatitudes, a section of Jesus' famous Sermon on the Mount. The Beatitudes are a list of blessings pronounced by the Son of God. In this verse, Jesus teaches us three things.

1. *Solace is possible to those who are broken by the loss of a loved one.* The words of Matthew are a blessed assurance to those in deep anguish. Though we may not feel the Lord's presence during such a time, that is when He draws closest to us.

2. *God recognizes your suffering.* We so often believe Father to be this faraway presence who cannot possibly understand the depths of our sorrow. God knows firsthand what it means to lose a

child. Your pain is real to Him, and He desires to wrap you tightly in His mighty arms of comfort and peace.

3. *You can be blessed in grief.* If we choose to cling to Jesus during the darkness of a devastating loss, we will recognize the blessing of Papa's promise to console us in our time of need. Discerning this kind of blessing takes time, beloved! But make no mistake, His care for you is His divine grace.

Oftentimes, the process of mourning is compounded by feelings of guilt or failure. Remember, friend, our enemy, Satan, will seize on our darkest moments. If the devil can keep us in a place of sorrow and condemnation, he can keep us from experiencing God's goodness in our most vulnerable seasons. Friend, our Mighty Father is greater than this petty thief. If we trust Jesus with our grief, we are blessed by His comfort and compassion, His protection and help. He takes us into His arms when we take the treacherous journey through the darkest corners of the valley.

MEDITATION:

On this day of meditation and prayer, let's reflect on the words of Matthew 5:4. As we enter God's holy presence, let us open our hearts to His gentle mercy.

Go into your quiet place with God. Breathe deeply and slowly. Imagine your lungs slowly filling with Father's healing presence. Pay attention to what you might be feeling. Is there any tightness in your body – your neck, shoulders, legs? Keep breathing and slowly relax your limbs.

Visualize yourself back in that place of pain – that hospital room, that crash site, alone in your living room, or standing over your loved one's grave. The tears are flowing when Jesus begins to gently wipe your face with His holy hands. He is so close to you, and as you inhale, the fragrance of His presence radiates through your pores. With every breath, the Holy Spirit overwhelms and consumes you, as if fresh waters are rising up from the deepest parts of your soul. As He pulls you close, He whispers, "My Father experienced this very pain. He sees your suffering, and it breaks His heart. Just as I am with My Father, you, too, will be reunited with your loved one again. For now, lean on Me, trust Me with your sorrow, and let Me make you whole again."

PRAY WITH ME...

Father,

I know You were there as I grieved my loss. I believe in my darkest moment, You held me and are holding me right now. But I still feel as if I am drowning in despair! My grief hurts physically – the pain is deep in my bones. Everything seems hopeless, and I simply do not understand. But I am choosing to trust You, O God. Blessed am I who mourns, for You are comforting me. May I sense your nearness in a supernatural way today.

Amen.

Day Fifteen

BRIAN'S STORY: BETTER THAN YOU THINK YOU ARE

Brian stood in the frigid hospital hallway and watched in shock as a middle-aged stranger in a white coat spoke words he could not hear or comprehend. He was replaying his last conversation with his wife, Liz, in his head. They confirmed their plans for the evening and kissed each other goodbye. She went biking, since she was training to compete in a triathlon, and he left for his regular Saturday golf game.

"This is a terrible mistake," he thought.

The man in the white coat led him down a long hallway crowded with food carts, gurneys, and medical staff rushing about their business. Brian trailed behind the man into a spacious room with pale white walls. As the man drew back the faded blue curtain, the sound of the rings screeching against the metal track over his head ripped Brian from his daze. There she was, his beautiful, young wife of four years. Blood stained her vibrant red locks. Her porcelain skin and rosy, freckled cheeks were covered in deep purple welts. Her face was swollen, and her arms were covered in scratches and more dark bruises. All of this the result of a truck ramming into the back of her bicycle and tossing her several feet into the air. The man explained she was likely killed on impact. It was all too much, and the smell of blood forced him to take a step back.

He looked up and noticed the monitors and machines were dark and as still and silent as his wife, and with that, he grabbed the first machine he could reach and flung it across the room. The deafening crash was no match for the sound of his anguish. He sobbed loudly and screamed, "No, no, no," over and over again as if it would bring her back. With Liz's passing went Brian's plans for a family, his hopes, and dreams for a future.

In the months that followed, he drifted away into a silent and stoic despair. His mother, Tish, spent months with him, quietly asking God to let her hear Brian laugh again. On one particular afternoon, he and his mother sat together on the couch. The roar of Pittsburgh Steelers fans echoed from the television when Tish took his hand and said, "Son, you are doing better than you think you are."

He was quietly outraged. "How could she think that?" he thought. But before he could scream, he swallowed the words and stared ahead as the TV drowned out his anxious thoughts. Brian went on to leave his thriving career as a software engineer – taking an early retirement. Months stretched into years, and the pain subsided, but his sadness and loneliness remained.

He struggled to understand why this was happening to him, and that question led him to a church just down the street from where he lived. Every time he attended, it seemed as if the pastor was speaking directly to him. In Brian's search for answers, God tenderly guided him to His Word.

"Maybe the Bible can help," he thought.

Within weeks, he was reading the scriptures every morning and regularly attending Sunday service. He would sit, take in the sermon, and observe so many seemingly joyous families around him, only to return to an empty house devoid of life and laughter. He often wondered if his loneliness and loss were anywhere on God's radar.

"God, have you forgotten me?" he began asking during his morning devotional.

Friend, do you believe that Father has forgotten all about you? Is it difficult to see or sense His presence in your grief? Not only does Jesus understand what you are going through, He is deeply moved by your grief!

The Bible includes several accounts of Jesus' reaction to His children's suffering. He wept when He witnessed Mary and Martha's anguish over the loss of their brother Lazarus (John 11:1-44 NLT) – visibly revealing His empathy and willingness to enter into our sorrow. Shortly after His resurrection, Jesus walked with two disciples who were grieving His death. He listened to their heartache and confusion, explained the Scriptures, and revealed how His suffering was necessary (Luke 24:13-35 NLT). This story illustrates His presence with us in moments of grief. But no other story depicts how intensely He identifies with human suffering than His moments in the Garden of Gethsemane. In Matthew 26:38 NIV, Jesus says this:

"My soul is overwhelmed with sorrow to the point of death."

This happened just before Jesus was arrested. He would soon go to the cross and knew what awaited Him. He was filled with the terror of the brutality that was coming. He understood the spiritual burden that loomed as He would take on the sin of the world, which would result in a momentary separation from His Father. He walked through "overwhelming" fear and anguish, and He did it alone. Be assured, friend, the Son of Man understands our suffering.

You do not serve a God who is emotionally blind and unavailable. When you grieve, so does Jesus. Remember, He is fully God - but fully human. This concept is difficult to comprehend and one of the many great mysteries of God. But because of His humanity, He can sympathize with His children.

Dear friend, I realize the loss of your loved one has left your heart shredded. You may be wondering if life will always be this painful. Jesus desires for you to take comfort in His promise to never leave your side. He is actually closer to you than ever before. Hold on, just as

Brian did, and have confidence in the One with the power to resuscitate your peace and joy.

Brian's days felt like years, but even in his pain, he began to understand the only way to survive the nightmare he was living was to grab hold of his Father's hand and refuse to let go. So, he stayed in God's Word. He prayed often. He persevered through the sorrow. Then, when he was ready, Father filled his home with laughter again. I know this to be true because I am his wife.

When we attended church together for the first time, four years after the death of his late wife, the pastor opened up his sermon by telling the congregation, "Friends, you are doing better than you think you are."

Tears filled Brian's eyes as He realized God's faithfulness.

Though Brian could never replace what he lost, God restored His life and mended his broken heart. Everything is different than he expected it to be, but he is happy and prosperous. He serves in his church's ministry and shares his story with others to testify of the God who weeps with us, heals us, and restores us from our brokenness. Beloved, God still has good plans for your life. Will you choose to trust Him?

PRAY WITH ME...

Father,

May I sense Your presence as I take in these words. Pour Your insurmountable comfort and peace into my spirit. Resurrect my faith, hopes, and dreams. Fill the empty spaces of my heart and show me Your faithfulness, O God! Help me seek a Christian community of believers who will speak life into all that feels lifeless. I know You weep and suffer with me. May I be reminded that You are intimately familiar with grief. Help me remember You are a good Father, and I am Your blessed child. In the name of Jesus.

Amen.

Day Sixteen

MEDITATION AND PRAYER: FATHER SEES YOUR SADNESS

"Weeping may last through the night, but joy comes with the morning."
Psalm 30:5 NLT

By the time King David wrote Psalm 30, he had experienced considerable heartache and brokenness. He lived as a fugitive for many years as King Saul hunted him down to try to kill him out of jealousy. He rose to power and became king after Saul's death, only to have his own son, Absalom, attempt a coup later on during his rule. He committed adultery with Bathsheba and conceived a son who died shortly after childbirth. David lived through several wars and lots of family drama. He also experienced the loss of big dreams. It was his life's goal to build the temple, a home for the sacred Ark of the

Covenant. Nearing the end of his life, he began to prepare for the construction of the temple, only to find out it was his son Solomon who God had chosen for this assignment.

Like David, you might be experiencing the death of a dearly loved one, the betrayal of a lifelong friend, the pain of a spouse walking out on you, or simply the disappointment of life not turning out as you hoped.

May you find comfort in the knowledge that Jesus is in our grief, and He is in the joy of the morning. If you know Him and keep your focus on Him, He says your weeping may last through the night, a few months, maybe even several years, but it will not last forever. You will see the sun rise again, and with that will come joy, peace, and the will to persevere.

Psalm 30:5 is a scripture that also reminds me of the resurrection. Everything went dark when Jesus was murdered and put in the tomb. With Him went the hope of the world for so many who knew Him and followed Him. But Jesus did not stay in that tomb. He rolled the stone away and rose again, and with that miracle came the promise of eternity, our salvation, and joy in the morning once again.

MEDITATION:

On this day of meditation and prayer, let's reflect on the words of Psalm 30:5. Together, we'll step into the realm of the Divine and feel His nurturing presence.

Sit and get comfortable somewhere tranquil, where you will not be disturbed. Breathe. As you inhale, imagine your lungs are slowly filling with God's hope and peace. Exhale distraction, despair, or anything else telling you things will never get better. If your mind wanders, acknowledge the wandering, then slowly bring your focus back to this holy place.

Picture yourself sitting with Jesus on the front porch swing of a quaint white house nestled at the foot of some glorious mountains. The two of you gently rock back and forth as the birds laugh and sing. The cool autumn breeze is no match for His overwhelming presence, which you feel penetrating your pores and filling you with absolute love. You both sit quietly and watch as burnt orange leaves fall gently onto the grass. But even with all this splendor before your eyes, your loss feels too heavy to bear. Sensing your grief, Jesus leans over and puts His holy hand over your heart. You cannot explain what is happening, but you can feel Him releasing healing power. As the tears slide down your face, you hear His voice.

"I love you, child. Let Me walk through this with you. Let Me hold you," He says.

PRAY WITH ME...

Precious Father,

I confess my heart is troubled and full of sorrow. Everything feels heavy and sad, but I pray for the Holy Spirit to fill this place. May I sense Your presence healing my broken heart. May I feel Your mighty arms tightly wrapped around me. O, Papa, help me through the night of weeping and grief. Hover in this place and fill the darkness of my heart with the light of the morning that You promise and only You can provide. Heal my heart and restore my spirit. I surrender my grief to You.

Amen.

PART THREE

THE BROKENNESS OF DOMESTIC ABUSE, ABANDONMENT, OR NEGLECT

Papa's love and healing power turns the ashes of abuse, abandonment, and neglect into a glorious testimony of restoration. As promised in Isaiah 61:3 NIV, "to bestow on them a crown of beauty instead of ashes, the oil of joy instead of mourning, and a garment of praise instead of a spirit of despair."

Day Seventeen

JACQUELYN'S STORY: HER FATHER'S EYES

Jacquelyn gasped for breath. She could not control the sound of profound fear and sadness that came from her body with every tear that fell. Mark stood in front of her and watched anxiously. As she struggled to find the words, she looked around at the white walls and funky zebra prints. This sweet little apartment was her first home, and it symbolized her newfound freedom from her parents. How painfully ironic that it would now be the place where she would lose her independence, innocence, and youth.

"I'm pregnant," she whimpered.

Dark shadows of rage and disbelief came across Mark's face as he questioned her.

"How could you let this happen? I can't have another kid. Is it too late to get an abortion?"

"I'm not doing that," Jacquelyn tearfully replied.

Though she knew her life was sinful, she was raised in the church and deeply believed abortion was not an option.

Jacquelyn always walked on eggshells with Mark, whose anger was unpredictable. He was already the father of a child conceived with another woman, and the news of her pregnancy pushed him over the edge in an instant. The expectant dad grabbed her by the neck and slammed her against the wall of her bedroom so hard he knocked the wind out of her lungs. His hands began to tighten, she could not breathe, and her legs weakened.

She slapped at his arms, but nothing loosened his grip. Panic filled her tiny frame as she fought for her life and the life of her unborn baby. In the midst of this terror, their eyes met, and she knew his face was not his anymore — it was eerily distorted. Mark's eyes were cold as onyx and radiated a chilling and wicked essence. Like pools of darkness piercing her soul, Jacquelyn knew she was staring into the eyes of the devil himself. Determined to live, she fought harder.

Then, just like that, Mark calmly released his hands from around her neck and walked out the door.

Something shattered in Jacquelyn that day. She left the relationship shortly after, but that demonic look in Mark's eyes and years of verbal abuse would steal her peace for years to come. After her son was born, she quickly learned to be a mom and fill-in dad, but feelings of worthlessness followed her. Every time she closed her eyes, she saw "his" eyes.

Struggling, lonely, and depressed, she began to evaluate her relationship with God. Jacquelyn knew Jesus was the answer - but she was far from Him. She'd walk into a new church and quickly notice judgment in the punishing glare of others – preventing her from returning. Something in her told her to keep looking until she finally landed in the place that made her feel welcome. This new church community became a family to her. She surrounded herself with men and women who became a source of strength and encouragement, and they loved on her son.

Her healing journey is far from over, but most days, she feels as though she is dancing in the warmth of God's loving gaze. The mending God slowly bestowed upon her spirit has blurred the memory of the evil she saw in Mark's eyes that day. Her spirit is full with the restorative peace, light, and love that can only be found in a relationship with our blessed Father. Today, Jacquelyn believes and lives out the words of Philippians 4:13 NLT.

"For I can do all things through Christ who gives me strength."

Jacquelyn led a Christian support group for single parents for a time and poured into her peers who carried similar scars. With the help of her group, regular therapy, the Word of God, and time spent in prayer, Jacquelyn feels more whole today than she ever was. Her son is a gentle young man who loves Christ and his church family. When life gets hard, and it does at times, Jacquelyn remembers what God has delivered her from and mouths the words, "I can do all things through my Jesus, who gives me strength."

Beloved, are you exhausted from carrying around the extra weight of worthlessness and shame – caused by domestic abuse? God gently asks you to leave it all at the foot of the cross, where He spilled His blood for you. That is how valuable you are to Him! When you feel like tapping out, He leans in and gives you more strength and more courage. He is crazy in love with you! You are His royal heir, and there is nothing that He wouldn't do for you.

Pray With Me...

O Faithful Father,

Forgive me for shouldering the blame for the abuse. I reject that lie today, in the name of Jesus. I trust that my feelings of shame and worthlessness are nailed to the cross. I embrace Your healing and redemption. I firmly believe in Your love for me and in the goodness You have in store. Gracious Father, I thank You for the transformative work You've initiated within me. I accept it all, in the sweet name of Jesus.

Amen.

Day Eighteen

MEDITATION AND PRAYER: FATHER SEES THE EMOTIONAL BRUISES

"The righteous cry out, and the Lord hears them;
He delivers them from all their troubles. The Lord
is close to the brokenhearted and saves those who
are crushed in spirit."
Psalm 34:17-18 NIV

It is believed that when David wrote this psalm, he was hiding out in a cave. He was a fugitive on the run from King Saul, whose jealousy drove him to homicidal feelings toward David. But we know David's story and how God delivered him from the murderous king over and over again. God was with David, and He promises to be with you.

Friend, you have endured tremendous trauma from someone who promised to love you, but instead, they hit you, pushed you, or called you worthless. God saw all of it; He has heard your cry and will deliver you from the heavy shackles of abuse.

You may think your life looks like a smoldering debris field of fear, shame, and unworthiness. But Father sees acres of lush, green land that He can reap a harvest from — He always sees the purposeful life that you were created for when He looks at you.

Beloved, Jesus wants you to know that His love will never hurt or demean you. His care is in no way rough or volatile but gentle and kind. His voice is a whisper, not a scornful shout of disapproval. You are the apple of His eye and He wants to transform your life, just as He did for David. Will you draw near to Him today?

MEDITATION:

On this day of meditation and prayer, let's reflect on the words of today's psalm. In the embrace of God's presence, we'll encounter the tender nature of His care.

Settle into a quiet and comfortable place. Begin to breathe deeply and slowly. With every inhale, imagine the sweet essence of God filling your body. With every exhale, let go of pain, shame, and the lie that you are irredeemable. When you are ready, close your eyes and picture yourself sitting at your kitchen table. Everything is unusually bright and warm, and you sense the healing presence of God all around you. Jesus is pouring His soothing salve over every wound you have carried when you suddenly realize He is seated at the table with you. The light around you gets even brighter and warmer.

You cannot see His face, but you sense His loving smile – Jesus is beholding you as He whispers, "I saw every moment. I know how much it all hurt. Now, stay close, child. I will redeem your suffering and make your life new."

PRAY WITH ME...

Gentle and Loving Father,

I believe You heard me when I cried out in fear and shame. I am confident You have the power to deliver me from all my troubles and that You are slowly mending my messy life. Give me strength and courage to face the difficult days ahead. Help me, Jesus, to keep my spirit focused on You. I commit my life and my healing to You. Pour healing into my life and repair all that is broken in me. I declare that I am righteous through the blood of Jesus. May Your mighty hand of protection come over me now. I love You and I thank You. In Your merciful name I pray.

Amen.

Day Nineteen

DR. NADIA'S STORY: YOU MATTER

Five-year-old Nadia sat across from her big sister's empty chair. She stared in shock as she watched the puffy Cheerios floating in pink milk, now tainted by her sister's blood. Her seven-year-old sibling quietly sobbed behind the locked bathroom door just a few feet away.

Just moments before, the two happily chatted and giggled as they picked at their morning cereal. Their mom moved busily about the kitchen as she prepared for work. To this day, Nadia cannot remember what it was that her mother said to them, but she recalls her sister responding in her typically sassy way. As the two continued their jovial conversation, her mother's hand appeared from behind her in a flash and struck her big sister in the back of the head with such force that blood began dripping from her mouth and into her breakfast bowl. She cannot remember if her sister hit her mouth on the table or what caused her to bleed. Nadia only remembers drop after drop of the crimson liquid falling from her sister's mouth.

Her quest for understanding led her to seek guidance from a therapist who skillfully assisted her in navigating the lingering wounds of her past. It took a long time and some hard work, but God tenderly guided her from a state of affliction to one of restoration. Nadia's journey unfolded from emotional defeat to triumphant faith.

"You matter to Jesus. He gave His life for you. He is able to destroy the chains of abuse that have kept you bound. Trust Him and get help," she says.

Little Nadia is now Dr. Nadia, the Christian counselor who believes that with the power of God, generational hurt from abuse and neglect can be reversed. She has broken those chains in her family, and you can too!

Christian counseling, setting healthy boundaries, regular time spent in prayer and the Bible, a church community, and support groups are all part of her prescription to a healthy life.

"Healing is a lifelong journey," she says. "I still struggle every now and then with my own inner critic."

When that happens, Dr. Nadia says a special prayer she wrote using her favorite scripture from the book of Philippians. This prayer helps to silence the voice of the liar, and she shares that with you to remind you that you do not have to stay stuck in unhealthy emotions.

Pray Dr. Nadia's Prayer With Me:

Dear God,

My thoughts often trick me into a corner where I am left afraid, hiding, or hurting. Help me to take my thoughts captive and line them up in obedience to You, Jesus. I am only human, but You gave me the will to choose. Help me choose to focus on "whatever is true, whatever is noble, whatever is right, whatever is pure, whatever is lovely, whatever is admirable—if anything is excellent or praiseworthy—help me to think about such things" (Philippians 4:8 NIV). Cleanse my every thought, O Lord, and tear down the things I think about myself that are not from You, in Jesus' name.

Amen.

Day Twenty

MEDITATION AND PRAYER: FATHER SEES THE PAIN OF YOUR CHILDHOOD

"You have seen me tossing and turning through the night. You have collected all my tears and preserved them in your bottle! You have recorded every one in your book."
Psalm 56:8 TLB

L ove, affection, and protection are fundamental needs we all crave from our mothers and fathers. Dr. Nadia's story of neglect and abuse during her childhood serves as a poignant reminder that we inhabit a world that can be sad and cruel. A world where the most vulnerable among us are frequently left unprotected.

When King David wrote Psalm 56, he was being persecuted by his enemies and in grave danger. Psalm 56 is a prayer of deliverance in which David expressed absolute certainty that God knew about the trauma and turmoil in his life. He declared the wicked would never escape God's judgment – he then goes on to paint a loving image of our Heavenly Father collecting and bottling up each of his tears. He did it for David, and He will do it for you!

Today's scripture is a promise – our Precious Papa witnessed every moment of abuse or neglect we may have suffered, and our tears matter to Him. Jesus left the glory of heaven to save us, and this truth should provide us with reassurance. The Son of God is on our side! His immense love and kindness is more than sufficient to heal any childhood wounds.

Dear friend, we serve a Father who waits for you to call His name so He can finally step into your life and break the chains of your abuse. You never deserved what happened, and you were never unlovable. Your abuser was wrong, and they will be held accountable one day. Jesus is gentle, kind, and He never abandons His children. If we invite Him into our emotional wounds, He is willing and able to begin the work of healing and transformation.

MEDITATION:

On this day of meditation and prayer let's reflect on the words of Psalm 56:8. Let's read it again. Then, join me in seeking comfort in God's presence. Let us trust in His tenderness, which awaits us.

"You have seen me tossing and turning through the night. You have collected all my tears and preserved them in your bottle! You have recorded every one in your book."
Psalm 56:8 TLB

Let this image of our watchful and caring Papa sink into the hidden corners of your heart. Breathe deeply and slowly.

Beloved, think of a time when you may have felt alone, unsafe, or neglected by a parent, grandparent, or guardian. How old were you? Try to remember where you were at the time. An empty apartment? A bedroom? Can you still hear your parents fighting in the other room?

KEEP BREATHING.

Your Heavenly Father is in your midst. The One who binds up the brokenhearted is with you. His holy gaze is fixed on you as you sense the intensity of His love. Picture the Father gently scooping you up in His strong arms. He assures you that every tear you shed is cherished in heaven and there is joy, peace, and healing ahead.

Linger here for a little while and listen as He whispers this message of love into your spirit.

"I would never hurt you, child. Do you know how much I love you? What happened in your home was not fair, and you never did anything to warrant what took place. You were a child, My child. The world is shrouded in evil, and I am sorry that it touched you. That was not

My plan. I long for you to experience My love and protection. Take My hand, let's begin your healing."

PRAY WITH ME...

Papa,

You know the childhood trauma that I have carried. Today, I surrender the scars and the wounds of my past. I bring before You my anger and every ugly word that was spoken over me by those who were supposed to love and protect me. I leave it here at Your feet. You say You love me, but I confess, oftentimes, I have trouble believing that. Please fix my unbelief. Let me sense Your loving parental presence with me now. I declare today that though my father and mother may have forsaken me, You, Lord, lovingly receive me and hold me close. Make me new, Jesus. It is in Your name that I pray.

Amen.

Day Twenty-One

CARRIE'S STORY: DADDY ISSUES

It was pitch dark inside the house as Carrie quietly walked in and locked the door behind her.

"Please, don't wake up, don't wake up," she thought to herself.

The graduating 18-year-old never violated her curfew. She was the good kid, the oldest of four, and the first in her family to receive a full scholarship to college. She was set to leave in just a week and wanted one last night with her high school friends, and her midnight curfew seemed so rigid.

"Surely, he can't be mad over this one time," she nervously wondered.

Just as she thought she was in the clear, her father's hand ripped through the darkness as it came across her face with such force she was knocked to the ground. The living room was black, and Carrie quickly jumped up and ran to the safety of her bedroom. But her father followed closely behind, threatening to beat her if she ever defied him again.

Carrie's mom stood between them and tried to calm her husband, whose face was flushed with rage. Carrie sat at the edge of her bed and sobbed. She wanted to walk out the door and never come back. That night was the last time her father hit her. She left for college a week later, excited to be free from his heavy-handed grip. But Carrie's daddy issues were just beginning, and she would haul that load of abuse with her for a long time.

Carrie excelled academically and professionally, but her relationships with abusive men gradually eroded her sense of self-worth, confidence, and everything else that contributed to her positive self-perception.

She settled for cheaters, liars, and the falsehood that if she were a better girlfriend, prettier, skinnier, or gave more of herself, these men would not treat her so poorly. By the time she approached her 30s, her self-esteem was non-existent, and she began to wonder, "Why am I alive?" Her thoughts got increasingly dark, and Carrie contemplated suicide at times.

Out of the blue, she received a call from a childhood friend. They had not spoken in several years.

Her friend was happy, and everything about her life seemed sound and wholesome. Nothing like Carrie's life – and she was drawn to her. At the end of the call, her friend invited her to church. Before she could think about it, she blurted out a nervous "yes."

of addressing all the physical, emotional, and spiritual pain you've carried with you.

PRAY WITH ME...

Merciful God,

Thank You. Thank You for saving, rescuing, and sparing me from the darkness that kept me trapped for too long. Thank You for crushing the chains of abuse. Thank You for deliverance. Give me courage to seek the help and resources needed. Give me strength to confront the things that have left me in desperate need of Your soul repair. Father, help me sense Your nearness, Your healing, and Your tender love — in the name of Jesus.

Amen.

Day Twenty-Two

MEDITATION AND PRAYER: FATHER SEES YOUR WORTH

"What is the price of five sparrows — two copper coins? Yet God does not forget a single one of them. And the very hairs of your head are all numbered. So don't be afraid; you are more valuable to God than a whole flock of sparrows."
Luke 12:6-7 NLT

When we experience physical abuse at the hands of a parent or someone who was tasked with caring for us, the brokenness of that kind of betrayal becomes deeply rooted in our spirits. Some spend a lifetime asking themselves:

"What did I do to deserve that? Could I have behaved better or done more? Am I a terrible person, unworthy of love and protection?"

Beloved, it's crucial to recognize that your worth has always been seen by God. Thousands of years before your birth, He chose to endure the cross out of profound love for you, His cherished child. Enduring the torture and humiliation of crucifixion, He demonstrated the depth of His love for both you and me.

Jesus empathizes with the pain you've endured, and it's important to understand that the hurt you've experienced should never have occurred. Your past does not define you. By inviting Jesus Christ into your life as your personal Lord and Savior and by asking Him to fill the empty places in your heart, you can find healing and restoration.

Moreover, as you embark on this journey of faith, remember that you are not alone. God's love is steadfast and unwavering, offering solace and strength through every trial. Embrace His love, and allow it to transform your life.

Meditation:

On this day of meditation and prayer, let's journey into the sanctuary of God's love. May we marinate in the words of Luke 12:6-7. Read it again.

> *"What is the price of five sparrows — two copper coins? Yet God does not forget a single one of them. And the very hairs of your head are all numbered. So don't be afraid; you are more valuable to God than a whole flock of sparrows."*
> *Luke 12:6-7 NLT*

When you are ready, close your eyes and picture yourself seated on the front steps of a picturesque beach house surrounded by wild sea oats piled high upon grassy dunes. You can smell the salt in the crisp, cool air and hear the mighty cries of shorebirds hovering over the water as they hunt for their next meal. Take a few deep breaths and quietly invite Father to sit with you.

Inhale deeply, then exhale slowly.

It does not take long before you sense the presence of the Divine beside you. As you bask in the warmth and love emanating from His presence, You hear His voice deep within your spirit. He asks you to look up at the birds again and reminds you, in the grand scheme of things, birds are insignificant creatures. Yet, God would never allow them to go hungry. As much as the chirping shorebirds flying over you matter to Him, they are nothing compared to you, beloved.

Papa goes on to explain that he mixed the very color of your skin and painted the shape of your eyes. He spent time creating the shade and texture of every strand of hair on your head. You are His most impressive masterpiece, and He is madly in love with you.

Though the one who hurt you did not see your value – our Heavenly Father saved you and kept you alive because you matter to Him. His breath is in your lungs, and the words of Luke 12, remind you that He is in control of your life and your future, but you must trust Him just as the soaring sparrows do. Jesus gazes at you lovingly, then He leans over and places a gentle, holy kiss on your forehead, and a warm breeze begins to blow.

Pause here for a while. You are in the presence of your Creator. Replay this vision and let God whisper more loving reminders to your aching heart.

Pray With Me...

O Perfect, Merciful Father,

Thank You for protecting me through the darkest moments of my life. Thank You for Your strength, resilience, and for bringing me this far. Lord, I believe You care more for me than the birds in the sky. You formed me in Your image, and I trust I am Your most valuable creation. Heal my hurt and confusion. Lord, guide the rehabilitation and rebuilding of my spirit. I receive Your healing over my life. In Jesus' name I pray.

Amen.

Day Twenty-Three

SHAUNDRA'S STORY: LEFT BUT NEVER ABANDONED

For as long as she can remember, Shaundra hated being told to go out and play, knowing she would see the man in the black pickup. Her body would tighten every time she approached the front door because she knew the familiar stranger would eventually pull up and park just two doors down from her house, where he lived with his *real* family. That stranger was her father, and he walked past her door nearly every single day for most of her life without so much as making eye contact with her.

Shaundra always knew the man in the black pickup was her father. It was no secret to his family or the neighborhood. She was mocked by other kids for being unwanted and the child of a woman with three other children from different fathers. Shaundra simply internalized the confusion and would tell herself, "One day,

I'm going to be someone and come back to find my father – one day, he will love me."

One particular day, she watched her father exit his truck and walk up to his house. His three children rushed out to greet him. They giggled as he teased them; they embraced and then walked into their house. From a distance, Shaundra observed and thought, "What a good daddy." This seemingly perfect image only forced her inside. She retreated to the darkness of her bedroom closet and wrapped her arms around her skinny knees. She murmured, "I never asked to be here — why am I here?" At just 12 years old, rejection was taking root in her spirit.

As the years went by, Shaundra transformed into a striking and sophisticated young woman who could grace the pages of a Ralph Lauren ad. Her designer wardrobe ensured she was always impeccably dressed. Despite the confusion of her upbringing and her father's rejection, she pursued success and perfection. However, after two failed long-term relationships, she realized she was still battling unresolved resentment towards her father. She was also aware that the path she was on would likely lead her to single motherhood, only perpetuating generational struggles. Raised in the church, she knew that if she wanted to heal, she would have to call on Jesus.

Emotionally starved and spiritually parched, she found a new church where she began attending a Thursday night Bible study. In that midweek class, she discovered a community that was unashamed about speaking truth in love about who God is and how He desires us to navigate obedient, godly relationships.

Shaundra would leave her Bible study in tears, week after week. She began to get some counseling, and it was clear that her Daddy in heaven saw through her expensive clothes and flawless facade. He was dealing directly with her heart and the wreckage of her life. Jesus was mending her childhood wounds of rejection, abandonment, and neglect.

Beloved friend, what childhood baggage are you attempting to mask with the right car, the right house, or the perfect clothes? God wants to peel back the layers of your hardened facade.

He says, "It's time to address your confusion and pain. Let Me repair all that is broken in you."

If Shaundra could go back in time and whisper a word of wisdom to that little girl on that front stoop, she says she would simply whisper the words from Luke 23, words that wrecked her and put her on the path toward healing.

"Father, forgive them, for they do not know what they are doing." **Luke 23:34 NIV**

Years later, Shaundra eventually came face-to-face with her father and forgave him. He never pursued a relationship with her, but she was able to put her painful childhood behind her. She ministers to young girls about the redemptive power of God to heal and transform all that is broken in our lives. She understands today that though she was left by her earthly father, her heavenly Father never abandoned her. He instead met her where she was and changed her life.

PRAY WITH ME...

Lord,

Thank You for knowing exactly what we need. When we surrender everything to You, You love us so much that You gently guide us to a place of deliverance and healing. Heavenly Father, I pray for those who are reading these words. Touch their hearts and soften their spirits so they may experience the goodness, the joy, and the wholeness of Your healing. Father, may they experience You in a supernatural way today. In the mighty name of Jesus.

Amen.

Day Twenty-Four

MEDITATION AND PRAYER: FATHER SEES THE REJECTION YOU EXPERIENCED

*"Though my father and mother forsake me, the
Lord will hold me close." Psalm 27:10 NIV*

This scripture hits closer to home than many would
care to admit. Rejection, abandonment, or neglect of
a parent is a betrayal that can have lifelong implications.
The scars of rejection are deep, intense, and often rooted
in our love and trust in someone who was supposed to
care for and protect us.

Feelings of rejection often lead to abandonment issues, difficulties trusting, and low self-esteem. Rejection
can make us feel alone in the world and have an abysmal

impact on our psychological, emotional, and spiritual health — and the enemy is counting on that!

Beloved, if someone in your life has rejected you, especially a parent, remember this: The Son of Man — Jesus Christ, was rejected and disregarded by His own people. Jesus knows firsthand what it feels like to be abandoned by those you love because it happened to Him. The very men who walked closely with Jesus, who were like brothers to Him, denied Him out of fear, leaving Him to face the cross alone. Through their actions, Jesus intimately understands the deep-seated pain that arises from rejection. He bore not only the physical torment of the cross but also the weight of abandonment by those closest to Him. Yet, in His suffering, He offers solace and empathy to all who experience the sting of rejection.

When David wrote Psalm 27, he was pursued by enemies he likely once called friends—men he may have served with under the kingship of Saul. The betrayal of their rejection became dangerous and even life-threatening for him. Rejection can threaten the quality of our lives, our self-worth, joy, and peace if we choose to let it go unaddressed. You can make a different choice today and refuse the enemy a foothold in your life.

MEDITATION:

On this day of meditation and prayer, let us enter God's presence and be moved by His compassion as we spend some time in the words of Psalm 27:10.

Think about a place you might associate with the rejection you experienced. Was it the front stoop of your childhood home? A closet where you hid your tears? Were you seated in your living room as someone you loved and trusted walked out on you? Visualize yourself back in this place. Is there a specific scent or smell that takes you back? Dig deep and linger in this place.

Take deep, slow breaths.

Inhale the love and acceptance of Jesus. Exhale and release rejection, neglect, and abandonment.

As you sit in this place, you feel hurt and confused. You begin to weep. As the tears fall, you sense the powerful presence of Jesus. He comes up from behind you and wraps His arms around you. Jesus is embracing you when you realize He is crying with you – you cannot explain it, but you just know He feels what you feel. He turns you around to face Him. His radiance is blinding. You cover your eyes with your hands, and Father leans in toward your ear and whispers:

"Though your earthly father and mother forsake you or reject you, I, the Lord, will always welcome you and hold you close to Me. This was never supposed to happen to you. They failed you – but I never will, child. "

PRAY WITH ME...

Heavenly Father,

Hold me close. Keep me in Your loving embrace. Heal me from the emotional trauma left over from rejection. Lord, deal with my heart and lead me to a community that will help me heal and transform my life for Your glorious purpose. Help me to remember that though others may leave me, You never do! Heal my pain, Jesus, I love You.

Amen.

PART FOUR

THE BROKENNESS
OF ADDICTION

In addiction recovery, God is a constant presence,
offering strength, comfort, and guidance as a compassionate and loving companion throughout the
journey. He reminds you, "Come to me, all you who
are weary and burdened, and I will give you rest.
Take my yoke upon you and learn from me, for I am
gentle and humble in heart, and you will find rest
for your souls. For My yoke is easy
and My burden is light."
— Matthew 11:28-30 NIV

Day Twenty-Five

RYAN'S STORY: GOD'S REDEMPTION

It was Labor Day, 2010, when police slapped handcuffs over 30-year-old Ryan's wrists. It was his third DUI in four years. He had partied so heavily in college that he lost his golf scholarship, and he spent nearly every day since then either drunk or high on pain pills. His parents were still paying for a lawyer who was working on Ryan's first two arrests for drunk driving. How would he explain this?

The smell of urine and sweaty grownups from inside his jail cell began to sober him up and made him anxious to get home. He finally got his turn to make a call and dialed his parents. He was relieved when he heard his father's voice as the recording announced his call from the Broward County jail in Florida. But before he could explain what happened, his father expressed his broken heart with one simple sentence.

"Don't ever call here again; your family is done with you."

It was an emotional punch in the gut, and all he could think was, "My life is over."

Ryan always had a special relationship with his father and considered him his best friend and hero. The thought of him walking away was a pain he could not bear, and he realized he was at the lowest point of his life.

Several weeks later, as he awaited his day in court, his father paid him a visit and lovingly asked Ryan to agree to professional help for his addiction. Several days thereafter, in what could only be described as a sheer miracle, instead of jail time, the judge court-ordered him to spend six months in a faith-based halfway house. That sober home became his sanctuary, the place where he finally broke free from addiction. Yet, a quiet determination burned within Ryan. He knew staying clean required more than just escaping the grip of drugs and alcohol.

He discovered a welcoming and supportive church with a Thursday night recovery group. Surrounded by fellow Christians, he received continual encouragement and prayer. Yet, the significant transformation taking place within him was rooted in his deepening relationship with Christ. For most of his life, Ryan couldn't fathom a future free from booze and pills. It seemed beyond reach. However, through his study of the Bible, he learned that true recovery was attainable through reliance on the guidance and strength of the Holy Spirit. He no longer carried the weight alone, nor did he attempt to maintain sobriety through sheer willpower. With Jesus as his constant companion, his strength was renewed, one day at a time.

As God's presence increased in Ryan's life, his temptations decreased. God gradually dismantled the walls that Ryan's parents erected to cope with his addiction, and what happened next could never have been predicted.

After his release from the halfway house, in their effort to support their son, his mother and father regularly attended church with him. Ryan's father, Michael, lost his own dad as a young man and long ago had walked away from religion. His mom was from a strong Jewish family. But the message of the gospel would not be denied, and it wasn't long before both of Ryan's parents came to know Jesus as their personal Lord and Savior.

When we recorded this story, Ryan had recently collected his 13-year sobriety chip. He reflects that when he looks at the chip, he sees the power of God. However, this milestone would be marked by something even more extraordinary. Just before Ryan reached this significant achievement, he experienced the loss of his cherished dad. Michael, a towering figure in Ryan's life, lost his short battle with cancer. Though his life was turned upside down, Ryan assured me that he had no desire to turn to drugs or alcohol. He could never betray the memory of the man who had loved him out of his addiction.

Grief dripped from Ryan's almond-colored eyes, his spirit visibly tattered. He sobbed heavily, gasping out the words, "If I had to endure it all again—the DUIs, jail, friends lost to overdoses—I would. Because my parents are saved, and my dad is in heaven."

Even in his despair, Ryan clung to gratitude and the truth of Romans 8:28 NLT:

"And we know that God causes everything to work together for the good of those who love God and are called according to his purpose for them."

Ryan is still mourning the loss of his dad. But he remains resolute in honoring his memory by ministering to other addicts seeking sobriety. He frequently shares about his recovery journey through the transformative power of Jesus Christ. He likes to remind those in the battle that "recovery without God is like taking a shower without soap." One can only imagine his father's radiant grin as he cheers on his precious boy from heaven's holy balcony.

Pray With Me...

Jesus,

I am a sinner, and I need You. Intercede in my recovery. I trust and believe You are the Son of God who went to the cross for my sin, and three days after You died, God raised You from the dead. I understand that no one deserves the free gift of salvation. So, I thank You for saving me. Now, transform my life! Redeem me from this haze and fill me with Your strength to stay sober. Holy Spirit, have Your way in my life. Heal me, God. I pray this in the name of Jesus.

Amen.

Day Twenty-Six

MEDITATION AND PRAYER: FATHER SEES YOUR STRUGGLE WITH SOBRIETY

"About midnight Paul and Silas were praying and singing hymns to God, and the other prisoners were listening to them. Suddenly there was such a violent earthquake that the foundations of the prison were shaken. At once all the prison doors flew open, and everyone's chains came loose."
Acts 16:25-26

The bondage of addiction is meant to destroy you. The devil uses addiction to keep you trapped in a cycle of toxicity, shame, and lack of self-control, preventing you from rising to the purpose God intended for your life. But just as God broke the chains that bound Paul and Silas in a Roman prison, He can crush the chains you struggle with today—whether they be alcohol, drugs, food, gambling, or porn. God can set you free.

What can you do today, right now, at this moment?

Get to know God, immerse yourself in His Word, seek professional help, and surround yourself with believers who will encourage you, pray with you, and support your recovery.

This road will be far from easy. There may even be setbacks. But the earthquake is coming.

Embracing the things of God causes the foundation of lies you've clung to start to rattle, and that rattle only grows louder as God tears down the falsehoods one by one.

As you worship, serve, and share about the goodness of God, a spiritual earthquake will shake up your life and loosen the chains that have held you captive. Worshiping God in a dark season, as Paul and Silas did, is powerful! So worship, dear friend!

If God could orchestrate a violent earthquake to shake the chains off His apostles thousands of years ago, He can tear into the addiction that Satan has used to claim your life! Do you believe that about the God you serve?

Jesus' resurrection power can keep you clean. One day, you will look up and realize decades of sobriety— but will you dare to declare the Lord's authority over your disease?

MEDITATION:

On this day of meditation and prayer, let's reflect on the words from Acts 16. Will you step into the company of the Divine, where you will encounter His strength, forgiveness, and grace?

When you are ready, close your eyes and visualize yourself sitting on the floor of an ancient, dirty prison cell. Roman guards stand at attention at the end of a long, dark, and dingy pathway lined with medieval torches. Flickering light sends shadows to dance along the cave-like walls. You look down at your wrists and see thick metal bangles connected to heavy chains tethered to the wall. You look a little closer and notice the words that describe your addiction engraved into the bracelets wrapped around your flesh.

Inhale deeply. Exhale slowly.

As this picture comes alive in your mind, you gasp as Jesus appears in your cell. His light is bright, yet His presence is calming. His radiance penetrates your body, exposing the places of hurt, pain, and shame that have kept you bound to those heavy chains. He knows exactly what drove you to that deadly habit, and He knows what it will take for you to be free from it.

He helps you to your feet and lovingly places His hand over your heart. His healing power immediately begins to work through your body, cleansing your mind and soul. Though you cannot comprehend how, He sends the cravings and urges from your flesh to the deepest pit of hell. The ground beneath your feet shakes violently, just as described in Acts 16. The prison doors swing open. You look down and realize the chains are gone. Then, your kind and compassionate Father takes you by the hand and leads you out of this prison—out of this addiction and toward your future.

As you stay here and meditate on this picture, settle into God's desire for you to sit with Him a while, allowing Him to begin His work in you.

Pray With Me...

Father,

I trust that Your power can liberate me from addiction. I will seek You, follow You, and worship You. As I lift my voice to You, O Powerful God, I declare that You are sending me the same earthquake You sent Paul and Silas. I am convinced You will violently shake and shatter the chains that bind me. Lord, You are my life-giver, and I know You will destroy this disease and set me free.

Holy Spirit, work in me, heal me, clean me, and save me. I make this petition in the name of Jesus Christ!

Amen.

Day Twenty-Seven

EVELYN'S STORY: A MOTHER'S PRAYER

"How can you do this to me? I hate you — I hate you," Emanuel shouted at his parents and sisters as police hauled him away from his apartment in handcuffs.

Emanuel was inebriated by another bender that began several days prior. He was caught drinking at work for the second time and was fired. He had not eaten in days. He was 136 pounds of skin and bones. He was dirty, disheveled, and his skin was yellow and broken out from the high levels of alcohol in his body. His black hair was overgrown, and his blue eyes seemed dull and devoid of life.

After three stints in rehab and more than a decade of alcoholism, Emanuel was tired. He could feel his body shutting down, and that only drove him to drink harder. He expressed his despair to an old high school friend who, in turn, called his mother, Evelyn. But this? Police?

This intervention was a betrayal, and his rage was like a hurricane poised to devastate everything in its path.

Before the police restrained him, Emanuel shouted curses and obscenities at his sisters. Evelyn brought his rant to an abrupt and surprising end with a swift slap to his face. In Emanuel's 47 years, his mother had never laid a hand on him or uttered a hurtful word. The connection they shared was sacred to them both. Emanuel was stunned. For a moment, their eyes met, and he felt the sting of her devastation. Before he could say anything else, the police wrapped the cold metal tightly around his wrists, and he began to scream and shout. His family could only stare through the apartment window in disbelief and pain as he was carried off for a 24-hour evaluation and then a fourth round of rehab.

For Evelyn, the choice was easy, but the pain was unbearable. Watching her youngest son hauled off in handcuffs was devastating. She had trusted God nearly her entire life and surrendered Emanuel to Him every day since his addiction became clear. But this felt different. This prayer warrior was hitting her own rock bottom. Still, it was all she knew to do. So, she tearfully turned to Father again.

Lord,

He was yours before he was mine. You formed him in my womb. I know you love him more than I ever could. Give him hope and strength to fight this disease, and do not let me leave this earth until I see Him serve you.

This prayer has been Evelyn's anthem for more than a decade. Being the mother of an alcoholic who suffers from bipolar disorder has taken its toll on her, but she continues to trust God for Emanuel's recovery and abundant future. She clings to the words of Psalm 37, especially the last two verses.

"The Lord rescues the godly; He is their fortress in times of trouble. The Lord helps them, rescuing them from the wicked. He saves them, and they find shelter in Him."
Psalm 37:39-40 NLT

Do you love someone who is sick with an addiction? Are you exhausted and doubtful that our Father can intercede in their life in a supernatural way?

EL ROI, the God who sees, wants you to know that you have captured His attention, friend. He weeps with you and sympathizes with your struggles. He understands the pain and suffering of a parent—He watched from heaven as Jesus, His only Son, was sent to the cross. The beauty of God becoming flesh is that He understands every single pain and weakness that we would ever suffer as human beings.

Beloved, He gently calls you to Him now. "Keep trusting, keep believing, keep praying. Deliverance, healing, and redemption is coming," says the Lord, your God.

Emanuel was doubtful this round of treatment would be different. Yet, somehow, in his deep despair, he found hope the size of a mustard seed — the very thing that Evelyn prayed for.

There is still a long road ahead, and every day is a battle. But, at the time that these words were penned, Emanuel celebrated two years of sobriety. He is healthy and committed to his recovery. Thanks be to God.

Pray With Me...

EL ROI,

You are the God who sees — I trust that You see how the weight of addiction has me worn and weary. Father, I ask You today to refresh and renew my spirit. Lead Your beloved child to the path of righteousness, and give me the strength to stay the course. Keep me from giving up and restore my belief in Your life-changing power. Lord, restore my peace and fill me with Your might to press forward. In the powerful name of Jesus.

Amen.

Day Twenty-Eight

MEDITATION AND PRAYER: FATHER SEES YOU AND MAKES YOU STRONGER

"For I AM the Lord your God who takes hold of your right hand and says to you, Do not fear; I will help you." Isaiah 41:13 NIV

Addiction strains relationships and has the power to destroy the sacred bonds of family and unity. It is natural for addicts and their families to experience profound helplessness. It is common to doubt that God is good or that He desires to help you or your loved one.

Friend, the Great Physician and Healer sees you. He sees the person in your life who may be struggling, and He promises you will never walk alone through the fires of addiction. With God, nothing is hopeless, and no one is helpless.

There is nothing that God does not see.

There is nothing that Jesus does not understand.

There is no trial that the Holy Spirit will not strengthen you for.

Father sees the pain of whatever it was that led to this addiction. He desires to intercede and bring you hope, healing, and rest.

MEDITATION:

On this day of meditation and prayer, let's reflect on the words of Isaiah 41:13. Come, let's enter into God's presence and be enveloped by His soothing care.

Make sure you cannot be disturbed. Take a few deep breaths and relax your body. Inhale the curing and life-giving presence of God. Exhale the darkness of addiction and desire for anything else but Jesus.

If your mind begins to wander, that happens and it's okay. Slowly bring your thoughts back into this quiet space with God. He will wait for you.

Picture yourself sitting in front of a serene lake surrounded by lush trees of every kind: balsam fir, sugar maple, aspen, and black pine. The bed of water is the color of emerald stones. You've never seen anything like this! The soft ripple of water gently kisses the shore. The birds are singing, the sun is on your face, and across the lake, you see a deer nuzzling her fawn. You hear the footsteps of Jesus walking your way, and all of nature comes to a hush. The King is here, and He sits right in front of you. The light around Him is radiant, and you cannot look away. He is magnificent. He gently places both of His hands over the top of your head. His warmth penetrates your body. Cravings, triggers, and lies from the enemy are all falling and submitting to the Almighty God.

"I AM purifying you," He says.

"I will make you stronger. I will wash away your weariness. I AM with you," says the One True God.

Linger here for a while.

Pray With Me...

Father,

I trust in Your sovereignty, Your strength, and Your goodness, which surpass any addiction. I pray, O Mighty King, that You would fortify my tired soul today. Infuse me with Your divine nourishment, and bring healing in the name of Jesus. Remind me that You, Lord, are guiding me through the darkness, holding my hand every step of the way. Show me, Lord, that I need not fear because Your presence and healing power is at work. I declare Your miracles are in motion, and I place my trust and belief in the possibility of recovery through the mighty and powerful name of Jesus Christ, my blessed Savior.

Amen.

Day Twenty-Nine

SAM'S STORY: POTENTIAL TROUBLE SOURCE (PTS)

Sam was barely in his 20s, and he was already tired. He was no longer smoking pot, but his pornography addiction was finally catching up with him. What began as a pastime at 11 years old had evolved into a dependency on lust that was shredding his relationship with a young woman he was falling for. It would take some time and an encounter with Jesus before Sam, a devout atheist, would acknowledge and understand that he was addicted to the salacious images.

Sam's parents divorced when he was a child. His mother was a product of hurtful church ideologies, and as he got older, he connected less and less with his father. Sam's moral compass was distorted and confused early on, and the darkness of X-rated material threw him deep into a hellish maze. Anxiety began to plant its roots in his spirit. But God, in His love and patience, was coming after Sam.

The relationship between this tall, dark-haired intellectual and his girlfriend thrived at first. They shared many similarities and bonded over their difficult childhoods. It wasn't long before the two moved in together, and Sam's addiction took center stage in their relationship. His habit began to tear at his girlfriend's insecurities. They argued about porn, created limitations around porn, and talked about it in couples counseling. But the bottom line was he refused to let it go. Desperate to save the relationship, the atheist agreed to go to church.

One service led to another and then another. They discovered a small church group of their peers, where they started building connections and forming relationships with other couples. Sam began counseling with a Christian therapist who helped him address his anxiety, one of the underlying causes of his addiction – and the thing he spent a lifetime attempting to numb. He and his girlfriend immersed themselves in the Bible and books by C.S. Lewis.

"Commit your activities to the Lord, and your
plans will be established."
Proverbs 16:3 CSB

Sam committed everything to the Lord — his time, addiction, and finally, his life. One night at a young adult's service, the pastor made an altar call, and Sam went forward and professed his faith in Christ. Imperfect, broken, and beautiful, He encountered the God who refused to give up on him. Jesus Christ was redeeming him. The former atheist learned that there is a higher and cleaner standard of living that has nothing to do with career, money, parties, drugs, alcohol, or sex. That standard is Christ, who created boundaries to keep us safe and healthy.

Sam and his (now) wife have created a healthy household for their precious daughter. They are committed to all that it takes to keep Sam in recovery. They've even created a code, Potential Trouble Source (PTS), for things that may trigger them so they can immediately address it. They believe that by keeping everything in the light with open communication, counseling, Jesus, and His Word, the future is brighter than they ever imagined it would be. Though Sam's resistance to porn is getting easier, he says recovery is every day, and he calls himself God's work in progress.

Pray With Me...

Heavenly Father,

I confess my struggle with addiction to pornography. Forgive me and wash me clean. Father, grant me the strength to turn away from this destructive compulsion. May Your Holy Spirit help me overcome the temptation. Fill my mind with thoughts that are pure, lovely, and praiseworthy. I pray for the guidance of wise counsel and a community of believers who can support me on this journey toward healing and purity.

Lord, set me free from guilt and shame. I declare today that all things are possible with You. Help me to walk in the freedom and victory that You have provided through the sacrifice of Your beloved Son, Jesus.

Amen.

Day Thirty

MEDITATION AND PRAYER: FATHER SEES THE BATTLE WAGED AGAINST YOU

"A final word: Be strong in the Lord and in His mighty power. Put on all of God's armor so that you will be able to stand firm against all strategies of the devil."
Ephesians 6:10-11 NLT

It is important to understand that addiction has kept you chained to a cycle of self-abuse that rendered you neutralized by the enemy's evil forces. The moment you choose sobriety, obedience, and to walk with Jesus, you become an imminent threat to the kingdom of the world.

Satan will do everything he can to destroy the purpose that God mapped out for your life before you were created in your mother's womb (Jeremiah 1:5). Once you decide to change your life, hell will come at you to imprison you again. The enemy wants you shackled to addiction because he hates you, and he hates God.

Beloved, you can beat the devil, and you can recover from your addiction. Not because of your own strength and who you are but because of who your Father is! He lives in you, and that means His power resides in you. The Lord and His army of warrior angels fight with you and for you.

But to succeed on the pathway to recovery, you must armor up to fight the spiritual battle that has been waged against your soul. Today's scripture from the book of Ephesians uses metaphorical language, which teaches you and me to equip ourselves with spiritual tools to resist challenges and temptations waged against us in the spiritual realm. I listed the tools of armor below for you to remember and use to combat Satan and his schemes.

- The Belt of Truth: Live in a way that reflects moral integrity. The enemy cannot thrive in an honest environment.

- The Breastplate of Righteousness: Fortify your heart with the truth of your righteousness in Christ, which must be evident in a righteous life that adheres to that truth.

- The Gospel of Peace as Footwear: Whatever challenges and temptations come your way, let the peace of God, rooted in righteous living, assure you that you are on the path of His will.

- The Shield of Faith: By trusting in the Word of God and acting on it, you can overcome anything the devil throws at you. Exercising your faith reduces the enemy's fiery attacks to nothing more than harmless sparks from a fizzling birthday candle.

- The Helmet of Salvation: Holding on to the assurance of salvation makes it harder to be deceived by the Liar, thus protecting your mind.

- The Sword of the Spirit: Utilize the Word of God (the Bible) as an offensive weapon against falsehood and evil. Do not live your life in defense. Beloved, pull out your Bible as a mighty sword against the enemy of your soul!

Enemy forces have been studying you for your entire life. They know you, your weaknesses, and your patterns. But the Lover of your soul, Jesus Christ, has already won the battle. The only power that Satan has is the power you give him. Read and study Ephesians 6:10-20 and remain grounded in the components of God's spiritual armor.

MEDITATION:

On this day of meditation and prayer, let's reflect on today's scripture. Step into the realm of the Almighty, where His strength awaits us.

Find a quiet place and ensure your comfort. Take deep, slow breaths to help you relax. If your mind wanders, ask the Holy Spirit to guide your thoughts. Focus on your breathing—inhale deeply and exhale slowly.

When you're ready, visualize yourself atop a mountain overlooking a vast, beautiful countryside. Below, two armies come into view. On one side, warriors adorned in luminous white armor stand, surpassing anything seen even in fantastical films. Their helmets bear a crest capturing God's sovereignty and power.

On the opposing side, fighters wear polished black armor. Each meticulously crafted chest plate bears intricate engravings that twist and coil like serpents in the shadows.

Heaven and hell prepare for battle over your soul when, suddenly, a bold trumpet blast echoes in the distance. Another army appears behind you, clad in the same radiant white armor. The celestial warriors part and King Jesus approaches. His crown gleams with thousands of brilliantly-colored stones, and His presence radiates power. He smiles, takes your hand, and reminds you:

"I fight for you, child. You are Mine. Armor up. This won't be easy, but I have already won!"

Pray With Me...

Mighty God,

You fight for me. Therefore, I will remain strong in Your power. Lord, I will ready myself with every piece of Your armor and remain under the cover and safety of Your wings. Teach me to stand firm against the strategies of the devil. Strengthen me and give me the courage to fight the battles ahead. Guide me, Jesus, to the path of restoration and redeem my life so that I may testify of Your healing. I trust and believe that this battle has been won in the spiritual realm, and You, God, will bring it to fruition in the physical realm. In the name of Jesus, I declare victory!

Amen.

PART FIVE

THE BROKENNESS OF MENTAL HEALTH CHALLENGES

In mental health struggles, God stands unwaveringly by our side. He tenderly offers comfort and support, as 1 Corinthians 10:13 NLT assures us that He faithfully walks alongside us. He promises that the challenges we face are within our ability to bear because we do not bear it alone. The Holy Spirit comforts us in our time of need and consistently provides a path forward, empowering us to persevere.

Day Thirty-One

HEATHER'S STORY: DO NOT BE DECEIVED BY THE LIE

Heather was just eight years old and missing a few front teeth when she pulled out her pencil and butterfly stationery to write her first suicide letter. Since then, the pain and compulsion to end her life have only grown stronger.

In July 2000, she frantically tried to kill herself inside her car in a South Florida parking lot. This was not her first attempt, but most volatile. Her deadly impulse filled her with supernatural force, and first responders hurried to tranquilize her, to stop her from dying. She awoke hours later in the psychiatric unit, woozy and restrained. Above her, the harsh glow of fluorescent lights buzzed incessantly.

Tears slid down her face; she was tired and intensely broken. Heather compelled herself to speak, and she pleaded with God to rescue her from that psych ward. In exchange, she vowed to dedicate her life to preventing others from attempting suicide.

Miraculously, a few days later, she was released and determined to keep her promise to the God who heard her prayer. She devoted herself to weekly therapy while doctors worked on her medication cocktail, which she believes stabilizes her. When she doubts God's goodness, she gets on her knees to pray. When she struggles with thoughts of death, Scripture is her sword. Her home is covered in Bible verses scribbled onto post-it notes, so when the enemy attacks her mind, she reminds herself of God's eternal wisdom.

Every day is a battle for her mind. She says, "When you want to kill yourself, you've convinced yourself of a lie." She says a suicidal mind is a deceptively dark place where so many of us make a permanent decision based on a lie, and the most common lies are contrary to what God says.

Lie #1: You cannot make it.
Truth:

"Do not be afraid, for I am with you. Don't be discouraged, for I am your God. I will strengthen you and help you. I will hold you up with my victorious right hand." Isaiah 41:10

Friend, the One who created the cosmos repeats in this scripture that He is with you and will strengthen you. You can persevere because our Father is beside you. Do not quit.

Lie #2: You would not be missed.
Truth:

"If a man has a hundred sheep and one of them wanders away, what will he do? Won't he leave the ninety-nine others on the hills and go out to search for the one that is lost? And if he finds it, I tell you the truth, he will rejoice over it more than over the ninety-nine that didn't wander away!"
Matthew 18:12-13

God cares about every last one of us! So much that His Word reminds us He will come after the "one" who is lost. You matter to God. He has come after you because He wants you to live. Do not quit.

Lie #3: You are replaceable.
Truth:

"What is the price of two sparrows — one copper coin? But not a single sparrow can fall to the ground without your Father knowing it. And the very hairs on your head are all numbered. So don't be afraid; you are more valuable to God than a whole flock of sparrows." Matthew 10:29-31

He knows the number of hairs on your head — He created the color and texture of your skin and the sound of your voice. There is only one of you. You are complex, beautiful, and special to those around you, but most especially to the God of the universe. No one can ever take your place. Do not quit.

Lie #4: You are not wanted.
Truth:

*"I have loved you with an everlasting love; I have
drawn you with unfailing kindness."*
Jeremiah 31:3

Beloved, God wants you to know you were always on His mind and in His plans! He wants to do so much with you and for you if you will let Him. He desires you and is drawing you near to Him now. If you feel like quitting, pick up the phone. Call someone — reach out! Refuse to believe the lies. In the name of Jesus, do not quit!

Heather is determined to stay alive, and talking about her disease has become another discipline. She runs to the suffering and works with first responders, training them to handle this delicate illness. She founded *WondHerful*, a non-profit organization focused on aiding individuals in mental health crises. To date, her group has packed tens of thousands of life boxes with essential tools to encourage and feed those who struggle, as she does. Because, as Heather would say, "One more suicide is one too many."

PRAY WITH ME...

Heavenly Father,

Rescue me from any thoughts that tell me to hurt myself. Help me to fight and cling tightly to Your truths. Give me the strength to reject the lies. Holy Spirit, nourish and comfort my mind. I believe that You are with me and will help me. If I wander away into the dark, You will come and find me. You say that I am special and valuable to You. I receive that, Father. Today, and every day that follows, I will declare that You love me with an everlasting love. I will fight to live, and I will not quit! In the strong and mighty name of Jesus!

Amen.

Day Thirty-Two

MEDITATION AND PRAYER: FATHER SEES THE TURMOIL IN YOUR MIND

*"Trust in and rely confidently on the Lord with all
your heart. And do not rely on your own
insight or understanding."*
Proverbs 3:5 AMP

Feelings and emotions are tricky. We live in a world that tells us, "Trust your gut, rely on your own instinct, listen to your inner voice." But what is one to do when experiencing the lows of depression, the panic of anxiety, erratic moments of PTSD, or the certainty that you cannot make it another day?

God's Word tells us we are to trust and rely on Him with all our hearts. When we find ourselves meandering through the depths of the valley, we must choose to silence our instincts and instead submit to the guidance of the Lord. Despite the hurt or desperation we feel, we must choose to trust God instead of ourselves and what we feel at the moment.

The darkness of suicidal thoughts, depression, and other mental disorders takes from us our ability to rationally process how the long-term consequences of our decisions will affect us and those closest to us. Heather says, "This is a dark place with no light." As she mentioned in yesterday's devotional message, "It is a deceptively dark place because what we are convincing ourselves of is a lie."

Beloved, do not risk everything for a lie! Pick up the phone and call someone. Open the Word of God and see what your Creator has to say. Go straight to the Source of Life and have an honest conversation with Him. I know your wounding is agonizing, and the struggle feels too great, but you are not alone! You are loved more than you will ever know, and you cannot be replaced. Fight, dear friend! One minute, hour, and day at a time.

Our precious Papa sees the war waged against your mind, and He will give you what you need to see tomorrow, and the day after that, and the day after that, in the name of Jesus.

MEDITATION:

On this day of meditation and prayer, let us enter God's sanctuary and experience His perfect peace.

Get comfortable in a quiet place where you can meditate. Ask the Holy Spirit to block out any thoughts or distractions that are not from God. Sit here a while. Inhale and exhale slowly and deeply. Imagine you are inhaling the truth of God's Word and exhaling any deceptive thoughts and lies coming at your mind.

Picture yourself in a garden maze at dusk. It's a bit difficult to see, so you put your hands out and run your fingers across the shrubbery. As you walk, the leaves and spiny branches tickle your fingertips. You feel like you've walked for hours. You take a right, then another right, and a left. You feel lost, confused, even disoriented. You are ready to give up and drop to your knees. Exhausted and weary, you cannot pray; instead, with every breath, you utter His name, "Jesus, Jesus, Jesus."

All of a sudden, a brilliant light appears inside the maze. You attempt to cover your eyes when you feel the hand of Jesus gently pulling you back to your feet. You look up and see the greatest love you have ever experienced radiating from the eyes of Jesus. "How is this possible?" you think.

He smiles and puts you at ease. "Come this way, child," He says.

He takes your hand and leads you out of the maze and into a breathtaking garden. The night sky lights up this place; it's enchantingly beautiful, and you feel alive! Butterflies and dragonflies are chasing each other, and the crickets are singing. Then Jesus leans in and says, "Trust me with all your heart. Do not lean on your own limited understanding. I will always show you the way. I love you, child. I love you."

Pray With Me...

Holy Spirit,

Grant me the wisdom to rely on You when the dark attempts to deceive me. Lord, when I am ready to give up, remind me of the maze. Light up the pathway and give me the strength and courage to trust You to lead me to a safe place. Breathe Your truth into my spirit and Your life into my lungs. Father, I am choosing to trust You when I cannot trust myself. Have Your way in my life now, Jesus. I love You.

Amen.

Day Thirty-Three

HEATHER'S STORY: WHY WON'T GOD HEAL ME?

Heather has been asking God to heal her mind and take away suicidal thoughts since she was eight years old. There have been moments when she wondered and asked, "Why won't You heal me, God?" Nevertheless, this woman of faith goes to the Bible for her answers every time and almost always lands on the story of the Apostle Paul.

Paul was a great man of God — as whole as any believer could be, but he was never healed of his affliction — the "thorn in his side." Friend, being made whole does not always mean healing.

> *"Three times I pleaded with the Lord to take it away from me. But He said to me, 'My grace is sufficient for you, for My power is made perfect in weakness.'"*
> *2 Corinthians 12: 8-9 NIV*

We are never told what Paul's "thorn" may have been. But whatever it was, Paul pleaded with God repeatedly and begged Him to remove his suffering. Paul's prayer was answered, just not in the way he hoped. Although God did not remove Paul's affliction, He gave him "His sufficient grace." The Greek word for "sufficient" is "arkeo" (ἀρκέω), which means satisfying or enough.[1] God was saying His grace or favor are enough — even satisfying.

Without afflictions or a "thorn" to wrestle with, it would be impossible to experience God's grace and power at work in our lives. In fact, for many of us, if it were not for the thorns, we would have no need for God.

Why God heals some and not others is a mystery, one we will know the answer to one day in eternity. For now, we choose whether or not we are going to trust God with the anxiety, depression, and all other disorders, the "thorns in our side," as Heather does. One of the biggest misconceptions in the church is that if our faith is big enough, God will heal us. If that were true, Jesus would never have suffered the pain and torture of the cross. He was overwhelmed with sorrow in the Garden of Gethsemane and asked His Father, *"If you are willing, take this cup away from me" Luke 22:42 NLT.*

Even Jesus got an answer to prayer that was not what He desired, which is why He understands our disappointments in suffering. He understands our weaknesses and pain and promises never to leave us alone through our darkest moments. In the depths of our sorrow and sadness, He nourishes us with His sufficient grace. He pours His power into us so we can make it to another day. Through the presence of the Holy Spirit, He provides peace that calms our anxieties. In prayer, He listens, responds, and lightens our burdens. Each of His promises in Scripture remind us of His love and faithfulness. Through support of fellow believers, He offers encouragement and practical help. In worship, He fills us with a sense of His greatness to bring us renewed hope and strength. Each of these blessings sustains us, demonstrating His constant care and provision.

Heather still prays that God will heal her mind. She longs for that day. Until then, she aligns herself with the Apostle Paul, proclaiming God's power, which sustains her life – and Heather is determined to keep it that way!

Pray With Me...

Jesus,

Despite the pain I feel, I will declare that Your Grace is sufficient. I submit myself to You, the One who gives life and takes it. May I sense Your nearness in my affliction. May I hear Your voice when my mind struggles and trust Your will above mine. Lord, I believe I will be healed one day. Until then, give me all I need to keep going. May Your mighty power work miracles in my weakness. In Your holy name, I pray.

Amen.

Day Thirty-Four

Meditation and Prayer: Father Sees Your Desire to Give Up – He Says, "Live"

*"Oh, that you would choose life, so that you and
your descendants might live!"*
Deuteronomy 30:19 NLT

For those of us who battle with depression, mood disorders, anxiety, and thoughts of suicide, the weight feels unbearable. The idea of ending it all becomes a tempting escape, and the compulsion that often follows can be emotionally and physically powerful. Friend, remember to say this out loud: "These thoughts and feelings are a lie." The words of Deuteronomy 30 remind us that God desires us to live "so that our descendants might live." Any thoughts and compulsions to the contrary are lies put there by the enemy or fabricated by a part of the brain that perhaps does not function properly.

Yes, heaven is awesome, and we all want to be there to experience perfection and rid ourselves of weighty and exhausting mental afflictions. But our Heavenly Dad has already determined the length of our lives. If God, in all His holiness and sovereignty, had a plan for the cosmos and the creation of humanity, He also has a plan for every moment of your life.

Some of God's most prolific prophets also thought of suicide. Job wanted an end to his anguish from the grief he suffered after the loss of his family and the decline of his health. The Lord said, "No," because He knew what awaited Job on the other side of his trauma. God showed Job so much mercy and compassion, and He eventually restored Job's life and all he lost.

Fed up and overwhelmed in the desert with His people, Moses asked God to kill him. God, again, disagreed. He didn't take Moses' problem away; instead, God blessed Moses with help to do the work he was called to do. God even generously fed the Israelites so they'd stop complaining.

Then there's Elijah, who ran for his life immediately following one of his greatest miracle moments as a prophet! Elijah prayed and asked God to let him die. Our kind and faithful Father responds with a tender "no" by feeding Elijah in the wilderness and nourishing him for the journey ahead. Again, God did not solve the problems these men faced. He showed them the love and support they needed to keep going.

Dear friend, your Loving King calls you to trust that He will give you everything you need for your journey ahead. He will make you stronger, and you will live.

MEDITATION:

On this day of meditation and prayer, let's ponder the words of the Scripture for today. Read it again and again. We will find God's gentle and caring nature as we embrace His presence.

"Oh, that you would choose life, so that you and your descendants might live!"
Deuteronomy 30:19 NLT

Find a quiet and comfortable place where you will not be disturbed. Imagine you are sitting at a large and extravagant dinner table. The wine glasses are trimmed in gold and sparkle before you, and the utensils are ornately designed and fit for a king. Piles of beautifully colored fruit, cheese, and other foods you have never seen before pack this perfect table.

Despite this incredible presentation, you are too tired and weary to eat. Your heart is heavy, but before you consider walking away, you realize the table is set for two. Before you can wonder why, Jesus appears. He invites you to eat with Him and takes a seat beside you. The aroma of Jesus' presence fills the room – His scent is sweeter than fields of fresh lavender.

You sit and talk for a while. You share your heavy heart with Him. He wipes the tears from your eyes, then cups your shoulders with His mighty hands. Healing power penetrates all that feels broken in you. King Jesus leans in and looks you in the eyes and says:

"I set this table just for you. You have not even begun to see everything I have prepared for you. I will feed you and breathe new life into you. I know it's hard, and you are tired, but you must stay at the table with me. You must live, child, so your descendants may join us at this table. I love you, child, and I created you for such a time as this. Take my hand, and let me lead you through this life."

Pray With Me...

Loving Father,

You are the Author of my life. You are the source of hope, joy, and peace. Give me the wisdom to seek help, the courage to endure, and the unbreakable faith that You will see me through every dark day. You have good plans for me written in the Book of Life thousands of years before I was formed. I declare today that my life is precious and good even with its difficulties, and You, God, are just getting started. I take destructive thoughts to hurt myself captive, in the name of Jesus, and make my thoughts obedient only to You. I come into agreement with You, Jesus, and choose life. Thank you for setting the table for me long ago, nourishing my spirit, and loving me.

Amen.

Day Thirty-Five

HEATHER'S STORY: THE WORLD'S JIGSAW PUZZLE

W hen these stories were written, Heather deeply grieved the loss of her beloved brother, Chris, and the unexpected death of her four-legged companion. Needless to say, she was visibly hurting. When asked if the Bible helps her get to the next day, her answer is unequivocal. Being in the Word of God is a matter of life or death.

Friend, you are a critical part of the earth's magnificent jigsaw puzzle, and your piece in this puzzle is irreplaceable. Heather explains it this way:

"God holds the universe's jigsaw puzzle box up in heaven. Every piece in that box represents a life He created, and it assembles into the most beautiful and complete jigsaw puzzle the world can even imagine. If you take your life, you remove that piece from God's exquisite puzzle, and there is not another backup piece in the box. You cannot bend another person's piece to fit the space where you belong. That is how much you matter."

Your place in the puzzle of humanity is unique in color, shape, and size. The same is true for your story of pain—it is different, and it carries purpose and meaning. Friend, it is hard to believe this when it feels like the dark cloud is ready to swallow you. But there is hope.

"The Bible can speak to you, even when you are alone and want to die," she said.

In times when she has made up her mind about living, her spirit reminds her of two powerful biblical truths:

"The thief comes to steal, kill, and destroy, but I (God) come to give you life."
John 10:10 NLT

"I will not die; instead, I will live to tell what the Lord has done."
Psalm 118:17 NLT

This scripture drives her to keep her piece of the puzzle on the table and in that earthly masterpiece. Amid the darkness of suicidal compulsions, she holds tight to the One who gives life and has the divine authority to take it. The power of God's Word rescues Heather again and again. She also combines non-negotiable self-care habits, like Christian counseling, medication, regular journaling, keeping healthy boundaries, and reminding herself of her worth. Nature is an important part of her daily routine as well. She gets outside, plants her feet on the earth, feels the sun on her face, and lets the breeze brush through her blonde locks. She says it is through creation that God shows her his tenderness.

"I'll get so desperate for a reason to live, and I'll express that to God and ask Him to show me something or give me something to keep moving. Then, as is my routine, I'll go outside and see a Chris bloom (from the shrub I planted in honor of my brother) or a sunset that takes my breath away. On one particularly difficult night, I looked up at the evening sky, and He sent me a falling star! It was the first time I'd ever seen that happen, and I knew God was speaking to me," said Heather.

Nature is her love language, and she believes that when she is honest with God, He responds to her and shows her His love and gentleness with the very thing that speaks to her spirit. Our kind and compassionate Father meets her right where she is and loves on her. Heather deeply believes God sees her and gets her through each and every day.

PRAY WITH ME...

Father,

My place in Your human jigsaw puzzle is precious and important to You. I am part of Your canvas of scattered fragments, and I pray for the Creator's hand to touch me and piece together my life. You love me enough to include me in Your plan for the world. Thank You for loving me so much! Guide my mental health journey. Lord, speak to me in my love language and reveal Yourself in a special way I can understand – open the eyes of my heart to recognize Your voice. Work in me now, Jesus.

Amen.

Day Thirty-Six

MEDITATION AND PRAYER: FATHER SEES YOUR UNIQUE VALUE

"For God loved the world in this way: He gave his one and only Son, so that everyone who believes in him will not perish but have eternal life."
John 3:16 CSB

Beloved, the God of the universe is madly in love with you. When depression or any other mental health issues arise to tell you that you do not matter, biblical truths tell a different story! Our Father is kind, and He values His children. Through Heather's story, we shared a lot of scripture with you. I pray that you will learn to love what the Word of God teaches us and be inspired by the truths God breathed onto the pages of that precious handbook for our lives. In promise after promise and fact after fact, we are reminded of our value to the Almighty. Take a look:

1. God loves you so much, He created you in His image (Genesis 1:27). You look like our Heavenly Father. You carry His holy DNA in your spirit. You reflect His divine design from your eyes to your fingers and toes, making you exceptional and precious to your Creator.

2. God loves you so much, He knows you intimately. Psalm 139 assures us that God did not create billions of humans, only to step away until meeting us in eternity. He took special care in our creation and knows we are "wonderfully complex" (Psalm 139:14 NLT). He knows your favorite foods, the things you dream about, and your fears. God spends time gazing at you, and His thoughts about us "outnumber the grains of sand" (Psalm 139:18 NLT).

3. God loves you so much that He takes great delight in you, He never turns you away, and He sings songs about you (Zephaniah 3:17 NIV).

4. God could not imagine heaven without His sons and daughters — without you. He sacrificed His only Son to save you. If you were the only person left on earth, Jesus still would have left His throne to die a painful and horrific death, only for you. Your piece of the jigsaw puzzle called humanity is essential to God and His Kingdom. Choose life, beloved!

MEDITATION:

On this day of meditation and prayer, let's take a moment to contemplate the words of John 3:16 and let us draw near to God's presence and behold Him for a while.

Get comfortable in a quiet place where you can abide in Christ.

When ready, close your eyes and visualize the perfect front porch. You are sitting on a swing and slowly rocking back and forth. A bright white balcony wraps around the minty-colored house with a dark teal door. The cool breeze combs over your face, and for a moment, you shut your eyes to take in the peace in this place. You hear the birds and the crickets as the sun begins to say goodnight. You open your eyes to a fiery pink, yellow, and orange sky. You step off the swing and go down the front steps. You are surrounded by fireflies lighting up all around you. You've never seen these mysterious creatures get this close. They are landing on your shoulders and pecking at you. As you giggle, you hear the voice of God. He is here with you. His presence is so powerful your eyes well up with tears.

"They're kissing you," He says about the fireflies. "Aren't they magnificent?"

"Yes," you respond tearfully.

"Beloved, I gave My only Son for you. That is how much you matter to me. I created every beautiful thing on this earth for your eyes. There are so many lovely things I planned for your life and so much for you to do, so live, child!"

PRAY WITH ME...

Blessed Father,

Thank You for creating me with the resilience to endure and the courage to choose life over darkness. Thank You for filling me with Your holy DNA, thinking of me as often as You do, singing songs over me, and most of all, sending Your precious Son to die in my place so I would live in eternity with You one day. Consume me, Jesus, and when I close my eyes, remind me of Your firefly kisses. Thank You, Jesus. I love You. I love You!

Amen.

PART SIX

THE BROKENNESS OF A LIFE OF SIN

In Father's infinite grace, He redeems those whose spirits are battered by a life of sin. In His kindness, Father promises you will find restoration, and He declares to you today, "Though your sins are like scarlet, I will make them as white as snow."'
Isaiah 1:18 NLT

Day Thirty-Seven

NINA'S STORY: WHERE I BELONG

Nina stumbled through the haze of Xanax and alcohol as she entered the Orange County Jail. She swapped her party dress for an olive green jumpsuit and plastic slippers, feeling detached from the process. A corrections officer led her to a cavernous room lined with bunk beds, its beige walls illuminated by harsh fluorescent lights. Amidst catcalls and overwhelming odors, her anxiety surged.

"I don't belong here," she thought.

Life could not get any worse than her DUI arrest. The look of disappointment and shame on her father's face the next day as he bailed her out should have been a wake-up call. Nina only doubled down on her "fun" life, convinced she'd earned it with a college degree, successful sales career, and hard work. Nina left jail angry at the police, her father, and herself, but her destructive journey was not over yet.

Nina was not a believer and leaned toward atheism. She was godless and empty and often felt like she did not belong anywhere. Her quest for identity and romance drove her deeper into the hookup culture, wild parties, drugs, and alcohol.

Rock bottom came years later. Nina was heavily in debt, had a job she hated, and struggled with anxiety and depression. Her romantic relationship was becoming abusive, and her boyfriend's involvement in a violent crime was enough to make her leave. She moved in with her brother in an effort to get back on her feet. One morning, he walked into her bedroom, looked at her intently, and said, "You are like Enron stock. You looked good for a while, had a condo on the beach, a good job, but you just blew up."

Nina felt the cracks in her fragile facade begin to give out. Alone again and feeling shattered, she did not know how to fix her life and couldn't see a step forward. Nina was like a ship lost in a dark storm without a compass. Once again, she belonged nowhere.

On her quiet drive to work that day, she remembered an old colleague, a "church girl" who constantly reminded her that she was praying for her – the party girl. The friend often told Nina, who complained about life, "If you want a sign, pray and ask God for one."

This was foreign to Nina, but as her tears came fast, so did her words, "God, if you exist, reveal yourself."

As she cried, a woman's voice broke through silence over the radio on a station she never listened to. The woman talked about her near-death experience and testified that God is real and heaven is a place. Strangely, Nina believed.

In the following months, she started having dreams about God, and her life slowly transformed. She began to journal – it was all she knew to express herself to a God whom she just met. She landed a job in South Florida and attended a Bible-believing church and its mid-week Bible study, which turned her life upside down in beautiful ways!

The Word of God taught her about a higher standard of living. She learned that the Father blesses obedience, which is meant to keep His children safe. She began tithing and serving and embraced a life of celibacy until marriage. Romans 12:2 (NLT) helped place her on a newly charted course:

"Don't copy the behavior and customs of this world, but let God transform you into a new person by changing the way you think. Then you will learn to know God's will for you, which is good and pleasing and perfect."

For the first time in her life, the ache of belonging was being filled. An exciting romance with Jesus was chipping away at her shame, guilt, and anxiety. A life of obedience was healing her from the inside out. It took time, tears, and the love from her new community, but our generous Papa mended Nina's life one broken piece at a time.

Do you believe Jesus can turn the rubble of your life into an exquisite work of art? God is able, and this is your invitation. The ache of belonging, that uncertainty; He desires to fill it.

One Sunday morning, Nina lifted her hands toward heaven and worshiped. The Holy Spirit swept over her, and she realized she was a long way from the nights she spent in a nightclub, high on ecstasy and other drugs. She was clean, whole, and free, thanks to her loving and faithful Father. As the worship team belted out sounds of glory, she thought, "This is where I belong — in my Father's arms."

PRAY WITH ME...

Papa,

If You are real, reveal Yourself to me. Teach me how to live and walk in obedience. Wash me clean and heal my brokenness. Forgive me, Lord, for my life of sin. I am accepting Your invitation – I belong to You. Help me to recognize Your voice and guide my journey. In the mighty name of Jesus.

Amen.

Day Thirty-Eight

MEDITATION AND PRAYER: FATHER SEES YOUR LIFE AND EXTENDS AN INVITATION

"Take delight in the LORD, and He will give you
your heart's desires. Commit everything you do
to the LORD. Trust Him, and He will help you."
Psalm 37:4-5 NLT

Some scholars believe that when King David wrote Psalm 37, he was in his later years. This psalm almost reads like advice an elderly David might have given his younger self. His words of wisdom and experience remind us that when we delight in the LORD, live for Him, and hand over the things we hunger for, God's desires become ours. But before that can ever happen, we must accept His invitation to follow, know, and love Him.

Do you remember what it was like to fall in love for the first time? Everything about this person was important to you. You may have even taken on their taste in music or food. You could sit for hours, listen to them talk, and share their deepest secrets. When we do this with Jesus, we discover a love that is intense, pure, and eternal. Falling in love with the Savior spurs radical transformation in our lives. Friend, Jesus desires union with you — oneness. He calls you to join Him in the secret place today. Accept His invitation and walk toward true belonging and freedom.

MEDITATION:

On this day of meditation and prayer, let's reflect on the words of Psalm 37:4-5. We'll enter God's holy presence and encounter His tender transformation.

After settling into a comfortable and quiet place, take a few deep breaths. As you inhale, God fills you with His grace. Imagine that as you exhale, you release guilt, shame, and all the ugliness of sin in your life. Hope is finding its way through your pores as you rest in the presence of the Almighty. If your mind wanders, it's okay. Gently bring your thoughts back into this holy place.

Picture yourself slowly hiking up a mountain covered in the coolness of lush trees and foliage. The scent of the forest is intoxicating; you smell pine, jasmine blooms, and sweet honeysuckle. You spot a clearing in the distance that leads to the summit. A silhouette emerges in the brightness of the clearing. As you draw closer, you realize it is our Heavenly Father, and He is waiting for you! As He waves you over to Him, you sense the power of His glory, and when you finally reach the clearing, you drop to your knees and begin to confess your sin. He smiles gently, leans over, and says, "Precious child, I forgave you long ago. You are mine, and I AM yours. I have washed you clean. Now, trust me with your life."

God is in this place with you, and as He begins to share His plans for your life, He fills the sky that surrounds this mountaintop with droves of dancing doves. Let's pray the words of this psalm, then sit still in the quiet presence of God for a while. As you remain in this secret place, remember that He is making you new one day at a time.

PRAY WITH ME...

Father,

Thank You for the gift of salvation. I am not worthy of what You have done for me, but I will live a life that makes You proud. I make You the Lord of my life. I take delight in You, and I release my heart's desires to You. I commit everything to Your mighty hands. Help me, O Gracious Father. All I want is to fall in love with You, as You did with me long ago. You are the Lover of my soul, and I will praise You every day of my life. I pray these things in the name of Jesus.

Amen.

Day Thirty-Nine

MADDIE'S STORY: GIRL WITH THE ALABASTER JAR

Maddie spent her whole life trying to please everyone, especially her father. But he was a hard man to make happy and could be cruel with his words. It was only when she did something "good," like pass a big test, prepare a well-cooked meal, or achieve a soccer accolade, that he showed her the attention and affection she craved from him.

Countless therapy sessions only solidified what Maddie had long understood about herself. She had become a woman yearning for the love and approval of her father. Seeking validation from her romantic partners, she would go to great lengths to please them, hoping for love, affection, and perhaps even a happily-ever-after.

Even after years of spilling her deepest secrets in therapy, she struggled with the shame of one-night stands, friends with benefits, and even adultery. She was haunt-ed by twenty years of sexual partners who easily discard-ed her. Maddie saw herself as dirty, cheap, and too used up to matter.

The only time she would feel relief from the weight of her past was when she attended Sunday morning services at a nearby church. A colleague invited her to church and only went once, but Maddie kept coming back. Her understanding of God was so limited, but she sobbed during worship, and strangely, it felt healing. It seemed every Sunday the pastor was reassuring her that God loves messy people and the church was a hospital for the spiritually and emotionally sick. Maddie consid-ered herself a patient in the ICU, and she was committed to checking herself in nearly every weekend.

Maddie stopped dating and continued counseling – this time with a Christian psychologist who helped her address a lifetime of feeling unworthy of love. She began to do life with her community of believers. Everything was changing, but it was her quiet encounter with God that rocked her. Maddie came across a story in the Bible: the woman with the alabaster jar (Luke 7:38-50). As she read this story, she felt God releasing her from the heavy chains of people-pleasing and low self-esteem that she carried all her life.

The Bible portrays the woman in the story as a "sin-ner," shedding light on her lifestyle, possibly indicating promiscuity or a life of prostitution. Upon learning that Jesus is at the house of Simon the Pharisee, she arrives uninvited. In a poignant moment, she kneels before the

Lord, she is overcome with emotion, and begins to weep. Amidst a gathering of religious hypocrites, she proceeds to anoint Jesus' feet with her tears and expensive perfume from an alabaster jar. She dries off His feet with her hair, then proceeds to kiss the feet of her Savior.

In the stunned silence of the room, Jesus admonished the Pharisee, clarifying that the woman's lavish act of anointing His feet demonstrated greater hospitality, love, and honor than Simon had shown Him. Jesus discerned that Simon's invitation aimed to challenge Him on points of the law rather than to extend genuine kindness or hospitality, a significant aspect of the customs of that time. The woman, whom Simon had silently shamed, now shamed Simon through her demonstration of genuine love and honor towards Jesus.

"I tell you, her sins—and they are many—have been forgiven, so she has shown me much love. But a person who is forgiven little shows only little love."
Luke 7:47-48 NLT

Maddie suddenly understood that every time she wept during worship, she was sitting and sobbing at the feet of Jesus – her tears were like perfume wiping His precious feet. Every act of obedience was an expression of love for a King who saw her, forgave her, and loved her back.

There are days when the enemy tries to remind her of her past. But she combats the devil's lies by rereading the passage in Luke, and she reminds Satan of the eternal damnation that awaits Him. These days, Maddie lives for the approval and validation of the One who gently and tenderly showed her forgiveness that transformed everything she believed about herself.

Dear friend, do you struggle to believe God has forgiven you and made you new? Trust today that Jesus wants to save you, not condemn you! As you sit at His feet, He whispers:

> *"Your sins are forgiven. Your faith has*
> *saved you; go in peace."*
> *Luke 7:50 NLT*

PRAY WITH ME...

Jesus,

I thank You for saving me, forgiving me, and making me new. God, I sit at Your feet with my alabaster jar. I trust You love me so much that You paid the ultimate price for my sin. Holy Spirit, transform my habits and what I believe about myself and show me who I am through the eyes of Christ. Fill me with the peace You promise Your blessed children. I love You, Lord. I declare Your healing over my heart today. In the name of Jesus.

Amen.

Day Forty

MEDITATION AND PRAYER: FATHER SEES YOUR REPENTANT HEART

"If we confess our sins, He is faithful and just and
will forgive us our sins and purify us
from all unrighteousness."
1 John 1:9 NIV

John the Apostle experienced a life of absolute fellowship with God. He traveled and ministered with Jesus. He watched Him heal and teach. John witnessed Jesus' death, resurrection, and ascension to heaven. John had a front-row seat to the life and power of Christ, which also makes Him an eyewitness to His mercy, grace, and forgiveness.

In the book of 1 John, we are lovingly reminded that the One who bore our sin is faithful and just. He forgives the terrible things we do and makes us clean once we come before Him and repent. Turning away from our sin is what true repentance looks like. But even though Apostle John reaffirmed this message, many of us struggle to trust its truth. We build altars to our shame and guilt and find God's forgiveness too extreme to apply to us.

Friend, if you believe your sin is too great for our Savior to forgive, it is because you have encountered the perfection of God. As He reveals Himself to us, we often become crushed under the weight of our own sin. Even the Apostle Paul referred to himself as "the worst of sinners" (1 Timothy 1:15). But instead of isolating and drowning in feelings of guilt and shame, which is exactly what the enemy desires, the Lover of our souls draws us near and invites us to experience a cleansing only He can provide.

The Scripture for today affirms God's forgiveness and reinforces His power to purify us from all unrighteousness – all that is wicked and evil. But when we choose to hold on to our past sin, mistakes, and regrets, it's like telling Jesus, "Thank You, but Your sacrifice on the cross did not cut it." Do not buy that lie, friend. Be free from shame and guilt and receive the peace that your Father wants to fill you with today!

May we be followers of Christ who regularly confess our sin and turn away from those things that keep us enslaved. Let us continually lean into the One who loves us so much He forgives our sin and wipes the canvas of our lives clean. The more we do this, the more we look like Him.

MEDITATION:

On this day of meditation and prayer, let's reflect on the life-giving words of 1 John 1:9. As we enter into His divine presence, let's experience the tenderness of God's forgiveness.

Find a quiet and comfortable place where you will not be disturbed. Take note of how your body feels, and let's begin by taking slow, deep breaths. Visualize yourself standing at the very spot where Jesus was crucified. You are in Golgotha, the skull-shaped hill in ancient Jerusalem. The wind is howling, the sky is gloomy, and You are standing on Calvary with Jesus.

Vivid images of Jesus' crucifixion flood your mind, and you cannot hold back tears. Standing beneath His cross, you confront the reality that your own sin contributed to the agony Jesus endured on this hill. Yet, in a gentle reassurance, He tells you He suffered through it all to redeem you because you were worth it to Him. Looking into His eyes, you sense a profound love unlike any you've ever known. As you gaze back at Him, you sense all shame, guilt, and regret slowly leaving you. Everything feels lighter. He smiles, delicately dries your tears, and says this:

"I paid it all. Right here, child. I conquered this mountain of sin and death to set you free. You were never meant to carry it all. So be free, child."

Then, He wraps you in His arms and whispers, "Let it go and trust all I have done for you. Don't you know how much I adore you?"

God sees your repentant heart — will you trust His gift of forgiveness?

PRAY WITH ME...

Father,

Forgive me for my unbelief and my doubts. Forgive me for my sin, which You bore. I receive Your gift of forgiveness and salvation through Your Son, Jesus Christ. I know I do not deserve what You did for me, but I am grateful. Thank You for loving me so much and deeming me worthy of Your sacrifice! I leave it all at the foot of the cross today, and I will walk in freedom and serve You all the days of my life. I love You, Savior.

Amen

Day Forty-One

LILA'S STORY: WEEDS TO SUNFLOWERS

Lila was your typical 15-year-old girl from an all-American family. Her perfect parents and spirited big sister were the center of her universe, and she felt lucky to have her familial bubble. But her sense of security was about to be shattered.

Her sister came home one day and grumbled about her mother's "suspicious behavior." Lila could feel the first pull on the thread that was holding her happy life together. Her sibling's questions to her mother got more aggressive by the day. She wanted to know where her mother was going, who she was with, and why she was talking to certain men.

One fateful night, the interrogation reached its climax. As Lila parroted her sister's cross-examination, her mother abruptly halted the escalating fury and chaos with a sharp, sudden slap across Lila's face. Time seemed to freeze as Lila locked eyes with her mother, only to find a stranger staring back at her. The woman she once admired, the nurturing figure whose affection she cherished, had vanished. Lila's mother swiftly packed her bags and left, moving in with her lover and leaving behind her husband, two daughters, and a multitude of unanswered questions. With the unraveling of one thread, Lila's life was transforming into a barren field of weeds.

To Lila, the pillar that held her life up was now shattered, and a burning anger ignited in her. In the years that followed that harrowing night, her insecurities amplified. She suffered from body image issues, feelings of abandonment, and an inability to trust or be vulnerable. She was convinced love did not exist and built a fortress around her heart. Lila wrote off marriage and settled for cohabitating with a handsome atheist named Adam. She was getting therapy and would frequent a local church, but never really committed her heart until she and her boyfriend began to struggle with a slew of issues, addictions, and lies.

Focused on preserving their relationship, Adam agreed to attend church. They started with Sundays, and to her delight, the gospel piqued his intellectual curiosity, leading him to absorb the "God stuff" one small dose at a time. They joined a young adult Bible study and found a handful of couples who became like family to them. Studying the scriptures revealed how loved and valuable they were to God. However, this spiritual discipline also brought Lila and her partner face-to-face with the question of godly obedience. She realized they needed to align their lives with the Word of God, and gradually, they surrendered their ways to His.

Their community posse talked them into taking a "Young and Married" class and lovingly encouraged them to consider marriage. It was not long before they were both baptized. Lila felt as if she was being wooed by Jesus! She realized the barren field of weeds, which represented her life for such a long time, was evolving into a meadow of bright and beautiful sunflowers.

Lila believes her Heavenly Father was gently digging up the roots of lies she spent years believing, and He was planting new seeds of His truth. The Great Gardener slowly and gently removed each weed from the field of her life.

In August 2022, Lila and Adam were married. God redeemed and restored her life, and for the first time, it was clear that though the person who brought her into this world turned her back on Lila and her family – Jesus never would.

> *"Can a mother forget the baby at her breast and*
> *have no compassion on the child she has borne?*
> *Though she may forget, I will not forget you!"*
> **Isaiah 49:15 NIV**

God's love is said to surpass that of a mother who helps sustain her child's life. These words are a tender and healing reminder to our spirit.

Lila forgave her mother, and they are working on their relationship. She says when she reflects on the last decade of her life, she sees her journey from darkness to light, lost to saved, broken to whole, and she is filled with a deep sense of awe and wonder for the Father who never packed His bags and walked out on her. Instead, He came after her over and over again. Thanks be to God!

PRAY WITH ME...

Precious Papa,

Thank You for never leaving me! You have the power to eradicate the lies I have grown to believe. I ask You, Papa, to do that today. Plant Your roots of truth deep within my spirit. Remove bitterness and anger. Give me strength and courage to forgive those who hurt me. Heal the wounds of divorce and abandonment from my heart.

Lord, You are my life's greatest reward. Thank You for rescuing me and redeeming my life from a future that was certain to be dark and without hope. May the days of my life be spent giving You the praise and glory You deserve. May the flowers in the field of my life continue to bloom, in the name of Jesus.

Amen.

Day Forty-Two

Meditation and Prayer: Father Sees Your Walk Toward Obedience

"If you are willing and obedient, you will eat the good things of the land."
Isaiah 1:19 CSB

Beloved, do you trust that God has the power to redeem the parts of your life broken by the sins of others? He wants you to know that life does not have to stay fractured and dysfunctional. God has a different set of blueprints for your life that are packed with purpose and so much good!

Do you trust Him enough to live your life in obedience to Him, abiding by the boundaries He created for you? The Lord is not a harsh and condemning God who desires to keep us from enjoying a good life. But he does create boundaries, as any loving Father would, for our protection. His boundaries help us heal from dysfunction or prevent it altogether.

The Bible tells us if we love Him, we will obey Him (John 14:21), and Jesus never asks anything from His children He hasn't already done Himself. He lived His earthly life in absolute obedience to His Father. Submitting to God's will is like igniting a stick of dynamite – God's power, provision, and protection are activated. He is generous to His children! When we live in devotion and obedience to Him, He engulfs our lives with His healing, transformation, and restoration – we will "eat the good things of the land!"

MEDITATION:

On this day dedicated to contemplation and prayer, let us pause to ponder the life-affirming message in Isaiah 1:19. Let's enter God's sanctuary and immerse ourselves in His gentle and nurturing spirit.

Find a serene space free from interruptions. Pay close attention to the sensations in your body and begin some deep breathing. Inhale obedience. Exhale defiance, temptation, and anything else keeping you from surrendering to our Father.

When you are ready, imagine the perfection of the Garden of Eden – a place free of evil and danger. Breathtaking, statuesque trees stretch out into the sky. You see fields of lavender, rows of brightly-colored tulips, and plump, exquisite fields of fruit that never existed on earth. The colors are more deep and pronounced in this place than you have ever seen. You have never been here, but you realize you have longed for this place since you were born. As you walk through the perfection of Eden, you hear the footsteps of the Divine. God is with you and His sweet scent is like a gentle and soothing embrace. Your senses are heightened, love and grace overwhelm you, and in disbelief, you ask yourself, "Am I really in Eden, with God?"

"I've created all of this for you, child," the sound of His voice interrupts your thoughts and sends you to your knees in awe and reverence!

"You live your life in obedience to Me, and I am so pleased with you. My abundance — My protection and peace are yours to take pleasure in, child." Jesus stretches His hand out to you and invites you to take a stroll with Him through this most blissful and intoxicating garden.

Pray With Me...

Father,

I trust that You desire the very best for me. Give me wisdom and discernment to live the way You have called me to live. May my life of submission be like a sweet aroma – pleasing to You in every way. Lord, I surrender the blueprint for my life, my selfish ambitions, and my dysfunction. I am willing and obedient. Release Your power in me, and may I bring glory to Your name, Jesus.

Amen

Day Forty-Three

MICHELLE'S STORY: FAITH, FORGIVENESS, AND FREEDOM

On an August night in 2011, Michelle and Xavier were driving home with their two toddlers packed safely in the back seat. It had been a busy day, but a good one. Michelle always felt grateful for her life, which she believed was as close to perfect as one could get. Her husband and kids were her whole world, but she kept Xavier on a pedestal. He was the man she always dreamt of marrying. Marinating in the joyful silence, Michelle opened up her phone, and what she saw made her body go cold.

It was a message from someone Michelle had never met, a woman who claimed, "I have been with your husband, and I am pregnant with his child."

In utter shock and devastation, she turned to the father of her children and said the woman's name. Xavier's face went white, and everything began to spin. Michelle screamed at him, shouted questions, then screamed some more. It seemed as if she'd entered an alternate reality as the street lights came at her faster and faster. "This had to be a terrible dream," she thought.

They finally got home and carried their sleeping daughters into the house, only to resume the screaming. It was a moment of debilitating chaos that stretched into three days of questions, tears, and Michelle's first panic attack. As painful as this moment was, God would not allow a single secret to remain hidden.

"People with integrity walk safely, but those who follow crooked paths will be exposed."
Proverbs 10:9 NLT

Xavier was raised in the church but had not seen the inside of a sanctuary in many years. Desperate to save his marriage, he scheduled an appointment with a therapist and found a church nearby. In the following months, they met with their marriage counselor during the week, and on Sundays, the wedded strangers sat side by side at church – each one silently praying for an answer to the mess of their lives.

One Sunday, the pastor gave a sermon about the cost of a broken marriage, and it was the first time that Michelle felt God was with her and He saw her. It was an intimate moment she shared with her Heavenly Father. After months of mourning the man and the marriage she believed were perfect, she felt God's light break through the dark, thick clouds of betrayal. In that light was a glimmer of hope she desperately needed.

Their Sunday morning appointment with God continued. During worship, Michelle would glance at her husband, whose face would be drenched in remorse. God was showing Xavier who he had become: a hardened man who surrounded himself with all the wrong people – someone who settled in sin and turned his back on God. As the Lord worked on Xavier's heart, the two began serving. They signed up for a "Love and Respect" class. They were both doing the work and praying for restoration.

One evening, after they tucked their little ones in and headed to their bedroom, Michelle felt the Lord tugging at her heart, and she knew it was time to say the words. She looked at Xavier, and her voice quivered as she said, "I forgive you."

Those words brought Xavier to a heavy sob of gratitude and spurred the mending of their marriage. They were becoming stronger and more united than ever. Through prayer, God's Word, therapy, and a church community, God was sealing the cracks of their broken union.

Soon after Michelle's forgiveness, they discovered the other woman was never pregnant. They were finally free to move forward as a family. Michelle believes the power of those three extraordinary words, "I forgive you," helped them turn a critical corner in their relationship with God and each other.

Today, when she thinks about all that happened, she can't help but be thankful for that painful text message that was meant to destroy her and their family. She is adamant that God stepped in and took the ugly trauma of adultery, lies, and betrayal and reshaped it for their good. Gone are the illusions of perfection. Gone are the pedestals painted by fairy tales we often tell ourselves. Xavier and Michelle are perfectly imperfect. The more they love Christ – the deeper their bond becomes. They boldly share their testimony out of gratitude for all that God has done for their family. It's their desire to give couples who are broken by infidelity the hope that they, too, can survive the devastation and even thrive if they are willing to do the work.

Pray With Me...

Father,

The pain is so heavy. We seek Your comfort and guidance as we navigate this difficult journey. Lord, we know You hate divorce, so give us the strength to do the hard work and grant us the courage to forgive. Help us rebuild all that has been broken. May our union reflect Your power to heal and transform the most impossible situations. As You bring everything to light, fill us with strength to work through it all. May we set our focus on You. We pray this in the name of Jesus.

Amen.

Day Forty-Four

MEDITATION AND PRAYER: FATHER SEES YOUR BETRAYED HEART

"He will cover you with his feathers. He will shelter you with his wings. His faithful promises are your armor and protection."
Psalm 91:4 NLT

Christians are taught to hold their marriages sacred. Out of love, obedience, and faithfulness to Christ, we often try to be intentional about nourishing the covenant we entered into with each other and God. So when infidelity is discovered, it shakes the foundation of all you hold holy and pure. To defile the marriage bed is to contaminate and pollute it, to desecrate and violate the oneness that is supposed to mirror Jesus' union with His church. The only way to come back from this devastating sin is through a genuinely repentant heart by the offender and forgiveness by the one who was wronged.

This message focuses on the heart of the one deceived. If you feel alone, God has never been closer. Your spouse may have betrayed and even abandoned you, but Father never has and never will. He invites you to hand everything and everyone over to Him. In this valley of despair and suffering, He desires to be the strength of your heart.

Beloved, He sees the trauma your heart and spirit have endured. He also sees what was done to you. Your life may feel like a series of aftershocks from the crushing earthquake of adultery. But just as earthquakes reshape land, God can reshape your heart, your spirit, and even (if both partners are willing) your marriage.

But first, Jesus wants to tend to your soul. He pledges to cover and shelter you with His mighty wings. His faithful promises serve as armor and protection over you. Your healing journey will be a long one, but the Lover of your soul wants you to know today that He will carry you the whole way.

In this season, remember to guard your heart against bitterness. The enemy knows you are vulnerable. Draw near to God and ask Him to help you. Immerse yourself in the scriptures and let Father remind you of just how much He values you. Do not do any of this alone. Stay in wise counsel and allow your community of believers to walk with you and love on you.

MEDITATION:

On this day of meditation and prayer, let's ponder God's promise of shelter and protection. He wants you to rest in Him now.

Find a quiet place to meditate. Close your eyes and begin to take deep breaths. Inhale tranquility. Exhale chaos and pain. As you relax, allow God's peace, calm, and rest to cover your tired and weary spirit. Linger here for a little while.

When you are ready, imagine yourself standing at the altar of a palatial church. The archways are covered in gold, and marble adorns the walls – the artistry is exquisite. There are white roses everywhere, and the fragrance is intoxicating. You hear angelic praises fill the air when you see Jesus. He is at the end of the aisle and walks your way. He is covered in light and love, so pure and perfect you begin to cry. When He finally reaches you, He wipes your tears and wraps you in a deep embrace. You sense His healing power and become instantly aware He is repairing your heart.

Then He whispers, "My covenant with you is unbreakable, child. You are my special masterpiece and perfectly created. I will cover you with My feathers. I will shelter you with My wings. I AM your armor and protection, and I will restore all that you have lost."

Pray With Me...

Father,

I am devastated, and this pain is crushing. But, I give it all to You. I surrender my despair, anger, and confusion into Your hands. Strengthen me, O Lord, and guide me through this season of healing and restoration. Grant me wisdom to navigate the many decisions that lie ahead. Thank You for Your promise of shelter, protection, and provision. Lord, fill me now with Your peace and allow me to sense Your presence. In Jesus' name, I pray.

Amen.

Day Forty-Five

JENNIFER'S STORY: DISNEY, DRUGS, AND DECEPTION

Jennifer's 2005 Magic Kingdom wedding was the event of the decade. The castle, horse and carriage, the characters, her dress, changing her shoes at midnight! It was the real-life fairytale she had always dreamed of, but her father uttered five words to her that ripped her from her fairytale long enough to realize she was making a mistake. Just moments before she walked down the aisle, as the music began to play and the chapel doors opened, her father looked at her and said, "We can still turn around."

At 26 years old, she wasn't fully committed to Christ, but deep in her spirit, she knew her father was right and that she was making a mistake. Regardless, the church was packed with people, everything was paid for, and she was intoxicated by her prince waiting for her at the end of the aisle. "This will work," she quickly convinced herself. She smiled, threw her shoulders back, and began her journey down the aisle and into a life she could never have predicted.

Life was blissful for a little while. But in 2008, they were hit hard by the recession. Jennifer's husband lost his job in construction, so he went back to his former career, dealing drugs. In a matter of months, he became a major east coast dealer of cocaine, pills, and pot.

Jennifer came from an affluent, Midwestern family, and this was not the life she planned. The wife of a drug dealer? Really? Still, she shared a young daughter with her husband, and she was determined to make the marriage work despite his illegal escapades. She turned a blind eye to most of his activities, yet the weight of his criminal lifestyle gradually unraveled the threads of her existence, leaving her to feel as if life was slipping out of control.

She was a new mom. Her husband was always gone and had an elaborate story for every absence. Jennifer could sense the darkness of her life and knew things needed to change. She often replayed that moment with her father on her wedding day, and the shame she felt hung over her like a dense, thick fog, which only distorted her self-worth.

Feeling profoundly alone, Jennifer deeply longed for her mother, who had passed away when she was just a young woman. Her mom would have known exactly what to say. Feeling trapped and unloved, Jennifer began to do something she had never done before: she started to pray. For months, she pleaded with God to change her husband. When that seemed like a dead end, she prayed a different prayer: "Lord, show me a sign. Just show me what to do."

Days after that critical prayer, she stumbled across an old cell phone in her husband's drawer. To this day, she can't say what compelled her to charge it and take a look, but she did, and what she found knocked out the final pillars that held her life together. Vulgar images and videos of her husband having sex and vacationing with other women flashed across the screen. She knew things between them were terrible, and their lifestyle was wrong, but this, too? Every limb in her body grew numb, but just as she felt on the verge of collapse, God's gentle reminder of her most recent prayer steadied her. "Lord, show me a sign. Just show me what to do."

This reminder felt like an answer to her prayer. Her Father was filling her with the courage and strength she needed to leave the marriage and the life she had settled for. Shortly thereafter and midway through divorce proceedings, her husband was busted dealing drugs and slapped with a 25-year prison sentence.

Embarrassed and deeply depressed, she sought therapy. It took years of hard and painful work with her counselor to understand how deep insecurities led her to settle for everything she knew was wrong. But it was her renewed commitment to her faith in Christ that shined a bright light into the darkest corners of her heart. Learning about the depth of Father's love transformed her mind and everything she believed about herself. Though therapy provided valuable support during challenging times, it was through Jesus that Jennifer found renewed joy and purpose in her life. Jennifer has finally learned to live in the confidence of 1 Peter 2: 9-10 NIV:

> *"But you are a chosen people, a royal priesthood, a holy nation, God's special possession, that you may declare the praises of him who called you out of darkness into his wonderful light."*

Jennifer has come to realize the depth of her worth to Jesus, finding in Him the strength to confront her challenges and raise her daughter. Through her journey, she has evolved into a formidable woman of faith. Happily remarried, she has found a God-fearing partner who stands by her in every aspect of life, embracing her daughter as his own with unwavering love.

She continues her healing journey with regular therapy and support groups. She and her husband lead marriage life groups at their church, and they also devote their time to helping addicts in recovery. Jennifer will tell you that the power of God is real: "He knew me, loved me, and helped me even when I did not know Him. I called His name, and He answered, like a loving and compassionate father would."

Pray With Me...

Blessed Father,

I feel as though I am too far for You to reach. Please, fill the space between us. Help me to sense that You are here with me and desire to help me. Father, Your scripture tells me I am Your chosen child, holy, and special. You tell me I belong to You. Lord, change my mindset and unhealthy ideas of relationships. May You be the standard of love in my life. Transform me, Jesus, and redeem all that is broken in me, in Your holy name I pray.

Amen.

SEEN

Day Forty-Six

MEDITATION AND PRAYER:
FATHER SEES YOUR
SELF-IDENTITY CRISIS

"Yet to all who did receive him, to those who be-
lieved in his name, he gave the right
to become children of God."
John 1:12 NIV

Friend, do you trust that Father cares about every single aspect of your life? The Scripture for today assures us of who we are when we believe in Christ as our Savior. We are His beloved children. Our Divine Dad cares about the difficulties we experience, the things that keep us stuck, and the way we see ourselves. Especially after trauma, sin, and every terrible thing that will touch our lives on this side of eternity. Friend, He sees the self-identity crisis you are suffering, and He says to you today, "Remember who you are, child."

The words in John are a blessed reminder of our place in the Kingdom of God. As His children, we are now joint heirs. His royal children! We have access to the One who calls us His own. This is a promise to you by our great God. But if you struggle with this, I encourage you to commit yourself to discovering your identity in Christ. This means immersing yourself in many of the spiritual and psychological disciplines that we have discussed on the pages of this book (prayer, church, support groups, the Bible, and therapy). Engaging in our faith practices helps us find strength, clarity, and purpose when we struggle with knowing our identity in Christ.

Focus on cultivating a deeper relationship with Jesus – align your thoughts, actions, and decisions with His teachings and example. Obedience is key, and as we line up our lives to His, everything will slowly begin to take shape in our lives, just as He planned.

MEDITATION:

On this day of meditation and prayer, let us enter God's presence expectantly. May we be moved by His care and compassion. Let us read the words of John 1:12 NIV in a different, more personal way. Think about writing this down and keeping it with you.

> *"Because I have received him, I believe in his name, and my Papa gave me the right to become His Child."*

We will never fully understand the magnitude of God's love until we see Him one day. But we can improve our understanding as we draw near to Him. We can find healing in knowing He claims us, He loves us, and He fights for us. Find a quiet and comfortable place where you can meditate on this scripture today. Take a few deep breaths.

When you are ready, envision yourself standing on a mountaintop. You look out and see miles of mountains and pine trees nestled into a dazzling sky. The sun is setting, and the evening canopy is captivating! The hues of burnt orange and fierce fuchsias have you mesmerized. You whisper, "Thank You for eyes to see this, God," when you suddenly sense His gentle hand on yours. You feel safe and loved. You stand there together for a while, then Jesus points to the vast land before you. As you admire the grandeur, He tenderly reminds you, "I love you beyond all this, child. I see you. I see your struggle to trust Me and all I have promised you. May My Word and My love run through you like rivers of living water. You are mine, child, and I AM yours. Trust Me and discover your identity in Me."

Then, the God of the Universe leans over and places a gentle kiss on the side of your head – His love is unimaginable; it is pure, real, and it never hurts or betrays us. Will you trust that He is your loving Father and you are His precious child?

Pray With Me...

Father, Jesus, Holy Spirit,

I surrender my life to You; my thoughts, my actions, and my trauma. I believe that You live in me and care deeply about every area of my life. I declare that You are my Perfect Papa, and I was chosen and redeemed by You – I am Your child. Therefore, help me build my identity in You. Help me to see myself through Your loving eyes, God. May I experience the fullness of every promise You have just for me. In the name of Jesus, I pray.

Amen.

PART SEVEN

THE BROKENNESS
OF INFIRMITY

In the anguish of illness, when earthly healing seems
distant, God's spiritual healing brings hope and
resilience, as Psalm 73:26 NIV reminds us, "My flesh
and my heart may fail, but God is the strength of my
heart and my portion forever."

Day Forty-Seven

LENORE'S STORY: THE BRAVE BATTLE

Chaos immediately surrounded Lenore as medical workers frantically wheeled her into the emergency room. She was hemorrhaging internally, losing a lot of blood, and knew she was in trouble. Suddenly, everything went black. She could not see or speak, but she could still pray.

"God, please bring me out of this," she silently begged.

This was the culmination of her seven-year battle with cancer. Lenore had already survived four surgeries, chemotherapy, a permanent ileostomy bag, dozens of radiation treatments, neuropathy, and daily debilitating pain. But she wanted to live, so she continued to pray.

"Please, God, bring me out of this."

She repeated these words in her spirit over and over again when something extraordinary happened — something she says is hard to describe with words. Lenore felt a supernatural touch that poured calm over her body and spirit. She could hear the panic in the doctors and nurses working on her. The beeping of machines was deafening. But there was no pain, no fear, just peace. Lenore could not explain how, but she was certain Jesus was in the room.

"It was almost euphoric. He touched my body, and I could feel His glory – His radiance. I could sense His nearness," she explained.

In the waiting room, Lenore's family prepared for the worst, but she defied doctors once again and awoke in the ICU a day later. The first thing she asked her husband for was a protein smoothie with an immunity booster to help her get better. There was little time to revel in this miracle, however, as doctors came bearing more bad news. The cancer was everywhere in her body. There would be no more therapies or treatments. They sent Lenore home with hospice.

"I've always felt peace about dying. I've reconciled with everyone. But if God lets me open my eyes another day, I am going to fight. If He gives me another day to live, I will accept that with gratitude. I am still here," she said.

What began as colon cancer spread to her pelvic area. At the time that this story was penned, Lenore lay in her bed, weak and ridden with disease. Wrapped in a black velvety blanket and propped up on a foamy pillow, she wiped the tears that fell from under her dark-rimmed glasses. Her olive skin was pale, her brown wavy hair was disheveled, and she regularly winced from the pain in her abdomen. Yet, she never stopped talking about how her faith in Jesus helped keep her alive seven years beyond her deadly diagnosis. This mother and wife still expected her miracle.

"Whether it's here or in eternity – God will heal me," she said unequivocally.

In the pain, grief, and brokenness that accompany terminal illness, Lenore remained radiant and hopeful that healing awaited her. Lenore's demeanor is a beautiful example of the words of Psalm 23:4.

"Even when I walk through the darkest valley,
I will not be afraid, for You are close beside me.
Your rod and Your staff protect and comfort me."

She says that Jesus has replaced fear with hope, and for the person reading this today, she wants you to know, "God doesn't always give a 'yes,' but that does not mean it's a 'no.' There is something further down the road that you cannot see. There is a divine reason why someone is spared and someone else is not. I beg you to listen to me and trust Jesus. He is the way, He is your comfort, and He is your cure."

Just one week after Lenore expressed these words, she peacefully went home with the Lord, forever liberated from the suffering and anguish of cancer. The very brave Lenore is finally healed and dancing in the presence of God.

PRAY WITH ME...

Heavenly Father,

We submit and surrender all illness and disease to You. Lord, we pray that You will strengthen those suffering through cancer and all other afflictions that seem hopeless. Father, we ask for Your healing hand over everyone reading these words. We declare miracles where doctors have spoken death. We receive hope and healing in the place of despair and sickness. You are the Great Physician. You are I AM, the God who sees our infirmities. Speak to the one reading this today and reveal Yourself to them in an intimate and powerful way. In The mighty name of Jesus we pray.

Amen.

Day Forty-Eight

MEDITATION AND PRAYER: FATHER SEES THE BATTLE IN YOUR BODY

"Is anyone among you suffering? Let him pray. Is anyone cheerful? Let him sing praise. Is anyone among you sick? Let him call for the elders of the church, and let them pray over him, anointing him with oil in the name of the Lord."
James 5:13-15 ESV

Do you trust that God can see the battle being waged for your physical, mental, and emotional health? Friend, sickness is a result of the fall. When Adam and Eve defied God in the Garden of Eden, their act of disobedience altered the condition of humanity and the world, leading to a state of brokenness, sickness, and death (Genesis 2-3). But through His sacrificial death and resurrection, we find hope in a day when we will never again experience the pain and sadness of illness and death.

James, the brother of Jesus and leader of the Jerusalem church, wrote the book of James more than two thousand years ago, but his words remain true today. He does not sugarcoat sickness by telling us that we will all be healed if we seek out our church community for prayer. That would mean that we would never die. He instead reminds us that there will be times in our lives when we might be too weak to pray, and that is when our church community becomes a spiritual lifeline.

In times of trials, our family of faith comes alongside us to pray, encourage, and lift us up. During a season of joyfulness, we celebrate together. Thank you, Father, for the strength and power in the Body of Christ!

MEDITATION:

On this day of meditation and prayer, let's reflect on James 5:13-15 ESV. It is in the realm of the Almighty that we will encounter His healing, comfort, and peace.

Take a few deep breaths and linger quietly in this place. Try to silence your mind and invite the Holy Spirit to join you.

Are you struggling with illness today? Imagine sitting in a hospital room surrounded by some of the prayer warriors in your life. Someone in the group touches your forehead with anointing oil. They gather around your bed, grab hands, and begin to intercede in prayer for you. You close your eyes and sense the atmosphere shifting.

Moments later, the room is filled with the sweet scent of God's holiness. As you open your eyes, you hear the faint voices of those praying, but you only see Jesus. He towers at the foot of your bed, too magnificent and radiant to see clearly—it's almost as if you are staring at a silhouette of bright light. You sense power, warmth, and compassion emanating from the light all at once. You don't want this moment to end; you want to stay here and behold the Lamb of God!

You finally hear Him whisper, "I'm here — I see the battle in your body. Take comfort in Me, child. I will hold you and walk through this storm with you."

Pray With Me...

Father,

I believe You have the power to heal. You equip doctors and are the true source of medicine, treatments, and cures. I trust that just as You numbered the hairs on my head and painted the color of my eyes, You designed the master plan of my life — I trust You. Lord, grant me wisdom to seek out the elders of the church to lay their hands on me and pray. Give me strength to worship and praise Your name, no matter what the diagnosis looks like. Holy Spirit, hold me during this difficult time. Show me all that You desire me to learn, and in my affliction, help me point the world to You. In the name of Jesus.

Amen.

Day Forty-Nine

AMANDA'S STORY: EXTRAORDINARY GRACE

In the early morning hours of August 20, 2021, Amanda shifted onto her stomach in her sleep, only to be jolted awake by the sensation of lying on top of a rock. In the darkness, her hand instinctively sought the source of discomfort, landing on a lump nestled within her left breast. In that moment, an unspoken intuition gripped her—she knew it was cancer and knew it was bad.

The following weeks were filled with mammograms, PET scans, blood tests, and biopsies. On October 26, just two months after her discovery, she heard the words.

"Left breast invasive ductal carcinoma," said the doctor.

It was stage three, in the lymph nodes, and aggressive. Amanda was not shocked by the words; she was simply numb. Her doctor explained that six rounds of chemotherapy and a double mastectomy awaited her, and in that moment, she decided she could not and would not let fear overtake her. Amanda firmly believed her life was in the hands of the God of the Universe.

"God, save my life," she prayed. "I want to see my children and grandchildren. Strengthen me for the journey ahead."

With Covid-19 protocols still in effect, she bravely attended her grueling seven-hour-long chemo sessions. Alone and terrified. Her designated spot was consistently the third blue chair in the chemo room, which sat beneath the comforting words of the Footprints poem. She would remind herself that she was not alone; God was with her, and He would never leave her side.

A few weeks after that first treatment, Amanda and her husband went on a short staycation to commemorate their wedding anniversary. She ran her fingers through her thick, blonde locks, as she often did, only to find heaps of hair in her hand. The reality of her illness brought her to tears, but only for a moment.

Determined that cancer wouldn't define her, Amanda courageously made the heartfelt decision to shave her head. She initiated the discussion with her husband and daughters. In a spontaneous and deeply moving gesture witnessed by their children, her husband, with tender resolve, took the clippers to his own head before gently turning them to Amanda's beautiful mane. Together, they shared laughter and confronted the uncertainty ahead as a united and resilient family.

Strong-willed and stubborn, she refused to show weakness or fear in front of her family, but as her double mastectomy grew closer, she quietly mourned. Her spirit often felt raw from the tumultuous whirlwind of emotions.

During Sunday morning worship, the week she was scheduled for surgery, she closed her eyes and belted out the song being sung by the praise team. Despite the uncertainty and fear that weighed her down, she offered praise to her Savior. Tears streamed down her rosy cheeks as she collapsed to her knees, overcome with weeping. It was the moment of profound release she had longed for. In that sacred moment, God saw her broken heart and met her exactly where she was. This was a deeply intimate encounter with God that she still struggles to put into words—but she says she felt held by God on that Sunday morning.

After a lengthy mastectomy and full breast reconstruction, Amanda embarked on her path to recovery, eager to leave this tumultuous period behind. She received regular PET scans and was cancer-free until March 2023, when doctors informed her that the disease had returned, only this time it was in her uterus, and she needed a full hysterectomy.

"How could life be so cruel? My breasts and now my uterus?" she thought.

She wanted to panic and scream at the thought of losing everything that made her feel feminine. Instead, she prayed, and the words of Deuteronomy 31:6 came alive in her spirit.

*"So be strong and courageous! Do not be afraid
and do not panic before them. For the LORD your
God will personally go ahead of you. He will nei-
ther fail you nor abandon you."*
Deuteronomy 31:6 NLT

Despite her devastation, she remained steadfast in her trust in the Great Physician. Amanda's faith in Him, who promises to watch over her, was unyielding. She struggled through several more months of tests, treatments, and preparation – finally, her uterus was removed.

Recovery was brutal. In her moments alone, she wept. Her body felt as if it belonged to someone else. She no longer recognized herself. Her scars were harsh reminders of all that was gone. But she stayed close to God, seeking His care and kindness. Prayer and worship carried her in her darkest of days and Amanda is on the mend, physically and emotionally.

She is a survivor who fiercely believes her loving Father would not bring her this far just to abandon her. She has years of PET scans to go before she is out of the woods, but her spirit is strong, and she becomes more courageous by the day!

"He holds the precise number of days in my life. He decides the end of my story. Until I see Him, I will praise Him and give Him glory," she declares.

Many who know Amanda call her "strong," but she says her resilience comes from her Father who held her on that day during worship and continues to carry her today. He promised to never let her go, and she has witnessed His faithfulness. Will you trust Jesus with your diagnosis?

Pray With Me...

Beloved Healer,

Pour Your medicinal power into my body and take away any infirmity or sickness. I need Your strength and healing for the journey ahead. Father, grant me the fortitude to face each day with the confidence that You are with me. I trust in You and ask for Your divine touch to bring healing, comfort, and restoration to my body. Remove all fear from my spirit, Lord. May Your will be done, and may I find peace in Your presence, always. In Jesus' name, I pray.

Amen.

Day Fifty

MEDITATION AND PRAYER: FATHER SEES YOUR FEAR

"For God has not given us a spirit of fear, but one of power, love, and sound judgment."
2 Timothy 1:7 NLT

The fear of cancer or its recurrence is undeniably real. Many mental health experts liken this fear to a form of PTSD experienced by numerous survivors. Enduring the onslaught of illness and coming face-to-face with death can leave one with deep anxiety, emotional triggers, and constant worry. In times of affliction, the Lord extends an invitation to surrender our ailments and fear of the unknown to Him.

The book of 2 Timothy is believed to be the Apostle Paul's final letter. As Paul nears the end of his life, he seeks to uplift Timothy in his ministry despite the formidable challenges they were both experiencing. Paul faced death, and Timothy was struggling with health problems, which made it easy for many to write him off. Paul encouraged his son in the faith to keep fighting the good fight.

Timothy, wrestling with an anxious spirit, is reminded that fear does not originate from God. Instead, the Holy Spirit equips us with His power, love, and sound judgment – everything we need to make it to the other side of illness, disease, and suffering.

Dear friend, God empathizes with your fears and anxieties. While the uncertainty of illness may seem daunting, you are not alone in this struggle. Lean on your church community, seek out a support group, or confide in a therapist who can assist you in processing the trauma, then entrust all your burdens to Jesus Christ, who fights for you.

Though we may not understand why sickness afflicts us or our loved ones, we can find solace in the certainty that God remains in control. He sustains us through the darkest seasons of our lives, guiding us to the ultimate triumph awaiting all believers at the finish line.

MEDITATION:

On this day of meditation and prayer, let's reflect on 2 Timothy 1:7. Come, let's step into God's presence, where His tender mercies await us.

Breathe slowly and deeply. Allow this breathing exercise to help you relax. Gently release worry and anxiety. Receive God's comfort and rest.

When you are ready, close your eyes and picture yourself walking through a beautiful forest. The giant trees around you shield you from the warm sun, preventing your body from overheating. A cool wind caresses the leaves of every tree and plant, and the smell of pine, wood, and jasmine tickles your nostrils. The trail is clear and wide, and you continue to enjoy this invigorating journey until you come to a fork in the lush forest. As you ponder the way forward, the sun begins to set, and the forest quickly grows dark. Afraid and unsure of how to proceed, you feel a gentle hand clasp yours. God is with you, and His radiance lights up the dark forest.

"I have given you all you need for the road ahead. No matter which path you take, My power will strengthen you through all that is unexpected. My love will protect you. My sound judgment will shower you with wisdom. I am the source of your life. Trust me. I love you, child, and I will never leave your side," says the Lord.

PRAY WITH ME...

Heavenly Father,

Your Word reminds me that I can leave all anxiety at the foot of Your rugged cross. I set before You my fears of cancer, disease, and death. I trust Your power to heal and restore me in Your time. Lord, fill me with strength for this journey. I declare that Your perfect love for me will cast out all fear, and Your power and wisdom will cover and guide me through this difficult time. I trust You, Jesus.

Amen.

PART EIGHT

HOPE AND HEALING
IN THE POWER
OF GOD

God's power is unmatched and sovereign over all creation. As Psalm 62:11 says, "God has spoken once, twice have I heard this: that power belongs to God." In His might, He upholds the universe and works wonders beyond our comprehension. O Blessed Father, how good You are indeed!

Day Fifty-One

THE POWER OF GOD TO HEAL, TRANSFORM, AND RESTORE

I was afraid of the dark when I was a little girl. But I remember thinking to myself, "Just relax. Your eyes will adjust." Soon after my parents would shut off the lights, my eyes would eventually recalibrate to the black of night. I still stumbled through the darkness on my way to the bathroom, and the shadowy figures that formed on my walls from the street lights still sent me to hide underneath my covers. Although the darkness distorted my view, if I sat in it long enough, I would eventually adapt to the darkness.

Trauma is similar. Trauma takes away our light, joy, and peace. It distorts our view of life and causes us to believe our surroundings will always be bleak and hopeless. The longer we go without addressing the trauma, the more our "eyes adjust" to fear, isolation, hopelessness, and despair. We become comfortable in the shadows of dysfunction.

In Mark 10, we read about a man who knew literal darkness. Bartimaeus was a blind beggar who heard that Jesus and his disciples were passing through on their way out of Jericho. Bartimaeus cried out, *"Jesus, Son of David, have mercy on me" Mark 10:47.* Everyone tried to silence and disregard him. But Bartimaeus shouted even louder, *"Jesus, Son of David, have mercy on me."* He finally made such a ruckus that Jesus stopped and had the man brought over to Him. I love what happened next.

> *"What do you want me to do for you?"*
> *Jesus asked him.*
>
> *The blind man said, "Rabbi, I want to see."*
>
> *"Go," said Jesus, "your faith has healed you."*
> *Immediately he received his sight and*
> *followed Jesus along the road.*
> **Mark 10:46-52**

In the same way Jesus set His eyes and attention on Bartimaeus, He is lovingly gazing at you and asking, "Beloved, what do you want me to do for you?"

The One with the power to heal, transform, and restore is holding out His hand to you. How will you respond? Do you want to see again? Do you need the Lover of your soul to cut through the darkness of your life's trials?

Bartimaeus cried out for the "Son of David." This was no mistake! The Jews knew that the Messiah would be a descendant of King David. He was publicly and boldly recognizing Jesus as the one true Messiah. In response to his great faith, Jesus healed the blind man and restored his sight.

Bartimaeus' healing underscores the power of faith and the love and compassion of the Great Physician. The blind man "received his sight and *followed* Jesus." This means he was transformed physically and spiritually.

Friend, do you believe that Jesus wants to heal you from trauma that has left you broken spiritually, emotionally, and perhaps even physically?

Immersing yourself in a community of believers is a good first step; Christian counseling is a must, but healing is never complete until you invite Jesus into the dark. He is gentle and kind, tender and careful with us as we surrender our pain to Him — The One who heals, transforms, and restores.

PRAY WITH ME...

Jesus, Son of David, have mercy on me!

Jesus, Son of David, I need You. I need Your transformative power to cut through the darkness and restore all that was broken in me.

Jesus, Son of David, breathe on me. Work in me and grant me the resources I may need. Lead me to the purpose You have ordained. Grow my faith and make me bold like Bartimaeus.

Jesus, Son of David, I receive Your healing. In the name of our Savior, I pray and declare these things.

Amen.

Day Fifty-Two

MEDITATION AND PRAYER: FATHER SEES YOU, AND HE COMES AFTER YOU

"Then Jesus told them this parable: 'Suppose one of you has a hundred sheep and loses one of them. Doesn't he leave the ninety-nine in the open country and go after the lost sheep until he finds it?'"
Luke 15:3-4 NIV

The parable of the 99 found in Luke 15 speaks to the fact that Jesus cares for the one lost sinner, and there is celebration in heaven when the one is found and brought back home. Beloved, this means that if you were the only person on this earth, Father still would have sent His Only Son to die a criminal's death on that old rugged cross, just for you. Yes, Jesus cares about everyone, but He loves to come after the one who has lost their way.

He treasures you!

God's love is the purest love we will ever know. Our finite human mind cannot comprehend the depths of His affection for us. Jesus is good, sacrificial, and perfect. Friend, you are His, and He is completely yours!

In the same way that the Great Shepherd is thrilled by the salvation of our souls, He rejoices in our growth, healing, and breakthrough. He cares about everything that happens in our lives, and because He *sees* us, He knows when we need Him most.

Father *sees* the pain left behind by trauma. He knows about your sleepless nights, and He hates the memories that trigger your anxiety and fear. We often need to be reminded that Jesus created the body of Christ — the church, the science of psychology and psychiatry, recovery groups, and even medication knowing we would need these resources one day. He considered all our potential needs and provided for every one of them, showcasing His love for us!

He sees you. You are not invisible. Though you've tried to isolate and run away from all that has hurt you, you have never been alone. The Lord cares about your healing. He revels in your transformation and is glorified when you are restored.

Jesus will never stop coming after you. If you put your trust in Him, He will tear down the lies you have believed about yourself. We serve a relentless Father, thanks be to God!

MEDITATION:

On this day of meditation and prayer, come with me, and let's enter the space of the Divine. May we sense his love and tenderness as we meditate on the words found in Luke 15.

Take a few deep breaths. Inhale God's transformative and redeeming power. Exhale indifference and unbelief.

Imagine that you are dragging around a large, dusty, and tattered black sack everywhere you go. It's too heavy to toss over your shoulder, so you continue to pull it behind you. Exhausted, you stop at the bank of an enormous river and let go of the sack so that you can rest for a while. There is so much life in front of your eyes. The water is moving so quickly down stream, the sound is dreamy. You notice a gentle breeze poking at the leaves on the trees. You pick up the scents of freshwater, wood, and wildflowers. As you take in the beauty, the wind picks up, and you close your eyes and smile in gratitude for this moment of rest.

You open your eyes and see a radiant figure seated beside you. Hundreds of brightly-colored butterflies fill the air around you. Dragonflies chase blinking fireflies, and the birds worship loudly in song. Nature is celebrating the presence of Jesus, and you are overwhelmed by this beautiful scene. The Lord finally stands and picks up the sack you have been holding onto for so long. It's packed with your hurt, shame, guilt, and everything else that has not served your life. Jesus empties the bag into the river, then tosses the bag in as well.

Father looks at you and lovingly declares, "Let it all go and allow Me to work in your life. I came after you because I love you. I refuse to let you go. Now, be free, child!"

PRAY WITH ME...

Heavenly Father,

I confess the bag I am holding is overflowing with triggers, sleepless nights, and immense pain. I often feel haunted by the things that have happened to me. Lord, guide me in my recovery. Allow me to experience a fresh revelation of Your love and compassion for me. Give me the courage to hand over this bag of darkness. It's been with me for far too long. I believe You have come after me and rescued me, and I declare Your freedom. Have Your way in me. I love You, Jesus.

Amen.

Day Fifty-Three

THE POWER OF GOD FILLS LONELINESS AND ISOLATION

"A person standing alone can be attacked and defeated, but two can stand back-to-back and conquer. Three are even better, for a triple-braided cord is not easily broken."
Ecclesiastes 4:12 NLT

Isolation is a common psychological response to trauma. When we are wounded by violence, loss, affliction, childhood abuse, or addiction, these deeply distressing experiences can overwhelm our ability to cope. Instead, we quietly withdraw from the world. When we are submerged by painful triggers, sadness, guilt, and shame, it feels easier to hide our depression or anxiety by isolating ourselves. Victims of trauma often lose their sense of identity and connection to everything and everyone around them, or we simply lose interest in the things that used to bring us joy and laughter.

Trauma has a way of driving us away from all that is good, healthy, spiritually nourishing, and that is exactly what the enemy, Satan, is betting on.

Dear friend, hasn't the Great Liar stolen enough from you?

I say this with utmost humility and care because I understand isolation. I've lived there before. Trauma leads us to believe solitude is a safe place. Friend, emotional wounds are powerful enough to distort the truth. Isolation can keep us stuck in our trauma and opens us up to spiritual attacks by the enemy, who's on a mission to keep us disabled, dysfunctional, and derailed from a path of purpose and victory!

The enemy helped drive me away from my family (my support system) for several years. The longer I sat in loneliness, the harder it became to get out. It almost felt like I was locked in a prison cell, and the key was beneath my own pillow the whole time. Despite knowing the key existed, I remained paralyzed, unable to unlock the doors of my mental and emotional prison.

Beloved, isolation is dark, lonely, and it steals our peace and joy. Isolation is a lie.

As my separation from the world grew darker, so did my thoughts. The profound hopelessness I felt led to thoughts of self-harm, and that was when I finally forced myself to do the thing I least wanted to do: call for help. The voice of the enemy urging me to stay put was loud, but with a sliver of faith, I took a critical step forward.

That decision led me to recovery. It changed my life, and it can change yours too.

Ecclesiastes 4:12 is the truth! When we stand alone, we can be attacked and defeated. But when we reach out and ask for help, the people of God step in and stand back-to-back with us to help us fight and conquer all that led to our captivity. When we allow believers into our pain, watch out! "For a triple-braided cord is not easily broken."

There is healing power in Jesus. He gently invites you today to take a step of faith. Heaven is shouting your name—it's time, beloved. I am cheering for you. Grab the key, and let's leave this prison of isolation!

Pray With Me...

O Loving Savior,

I ask You today to break through the darkness of my solitude. Make this place uncomfortable for me. Give me the guts to make the call I know I need to make and walk toward the healing that You desire for me. Lord, I bind up every lie the Thief has ever whispered to me and release peace, freedom, and courage into my spirit, in the name of Jesus. I declare that You have rescued me from solitary confinement and are leading me to a place of healing and hope.

Lord, guide my path, transform my life, and be glorified.

Amen.

Day Fifty-Four

MEDITATION AND PRAYER:
FATHER SEES HOW YOU
HAVE SUFFERED

*"Daughter, your faith has made you well. Go in
peace. Your suffering is over."*
Mark 5:34 NLT

The story of the woman with the issue of blood wrecks
me every time I read it. When I think of someone who
is lonely, rejected, outcast, or isolated, I think of the woman with the issue of blood. The Bible never tells us her
name, only what was wrong with her. She had an illness
that led her to bleed for 12 years. Scripture also explains
that she gave all she had to doctors, but her condition
only worsened.

Because she bled, she was considered "ceremoniously unclean" by her community. According to Jewish law,
blood was defiling, which meant this woman could not

worship in God's temple or touch anyone. Consequently, she was excluded from participating in religious events, she could not sit or eat with others, and she had to let people know she was unclean so they would not touch her. It's as if this woman with the issue of blood lived in a 12-year quarantine! Imagine how sad, lonely, and depressed she may have been. Consider how invisible she felt.

The Bible says the woman heard the reports about Jesus and went to see Him. Jesus was in the crowd when this woman risked everything to get to Him. She did not care who might recognize her or that she was touching other people. She needed to get to Jesus. The woman believed, *"If I could just touch His robe, I will be healed" (Mark 5:28).* When she finally got close enough, she reached out and touched his garment, and the Word says healing power came out from Jesus and she was instantly cured of her condition.

This "unclean" woman took a tremendous risk when she touched Jesus. She could have been severely punished by the religious leaders of that time. But her courageous act of faith resulted in her physical healing, and Jesus did not stop with that miracle! What He did next mended the woman's broken spirit.

The scriptures tell us the woman fell to her knees and trembled before Jesus, who had stopped to find out who touched Him. Our kind and compassionate King did not shun or admonish her for having the audacity to touch Him. Instead, He said to her, *"Daughter, your faith has made you well. Go in peace. Your suffering is over" (Mark 5:34).*

When Jesus looked at her, He never saw the "unclean woman with the issue of blood." He only saw His beloved daughter. He acknowledged her with a name that is full of affection and love. For someone who likely suffered the pain of isolation and despair for 12 years, this was like a healing balm to her spirit. He didn't just heal the woman's illness. He healed the whole person!

Will you dare to brave your fears? Re-engage your church community, make that call to a medical professional, or go into that secret place with God and recommit your life to Him? To say "yes" is to touch the holy hem of His glorious garment. Let your Father begin to address your suffering, friend. O, how He desires to tell you, "Your faith has made you well!"

MEDITATION:

On this day of meditation and prayer, let's reflect on this story in Mark 5. As we enter into the secret place with God, let us seek the warmth of His supernatural presence.

Get comfortable in a quiet place where it's just you and the Savior. Breathe slowly and deeply. Take in peace, tranquility, and healing. Release sadness, rejection, and isolation.

Think about the story of the woman with the issue of blood. Picture yourself standing before this massive crowd. Everyone is trying to get to Jesus. The atmosphere is chaotic and loud. There you stand, holding years of pain and sadness. Even with this crowd of people, you feel invisible, insignificant, and unable to move. Frustrated and scared, you close your eyes, and instantly everything goes silent!

When you open your eyes again, the crowds are gone. Everyone has disappeared except for Jesus. His eyes are radiant with love that you can feel to the very core of your spirit. You run to your Father, fall to your knees before Him, and touch the lower fringe of His royal robe.

Jesus delicately helps you back up, and you realize something is different. A warmth spreads through your body unlike anything you'd ever felt. The world seems brighter, the air lighter. A wave of peace washes over you, erasing the ache that became your constant companion. You look up at Jesus – his smile radiates kindness. He places His hand on your cheek and says, "I have seen your suffering, and I've been waiting for you, child. Today, your faith has made you well; now walk with me."

Pray With Me…

Jesus,

I am the person with the issue of blood. I believe You have seen my suffering. Lord, I am walking out of isolation and into Your arms of safety and comfort. Give me the courage to press through the crowd. Release Your healing power over me and transform my pain into purpose, in the name of Jesus.

Amen.

Day Fifty-Five

THE POWER OF GOD TO RENAME YOU

Have you ever been given a name, title, or label you never chose, only to feel shame and rejection when called by that name? We are taught to be careful with the names we call our children because we know that labels have the power to affect what an impressionable child grows up to believe about themselves. Yet, we are much harder on each other as adults. We are quick to tie words like head-case, addict, damaged, slut, or worse to those who bear the image of Christ.

Culture constantly tries to tell us where we fit or belong, and the world is good at loudly rejecting someone who has made mistakes or simply does not measure up. But I propose to you, friend, that only your Creator has the authority to name you!

In the book of Joshua, we encounter a woman whose label likely relegated her to the fringes of her community. Rahab was a prostitute whose home was built into Jericho's city wall, making it convenient for travelers seeking lodging and sexual favors. But it also provided an easy hiding place for Israelite spies. As tales of Israelite victories spread, Rahab learned of God's mighty deeds, including the parting of the Red Sea. Aware that Israel was coming to claim the land God promised them, Rahab, unlike the rest of her community, set aside her fear and boldly turned to the Lord for her salvation. She aided the Israelite spies, who, in turn, vowed to spare her life.

Friend, we serve a God who loves to use broken and labeled people like Rahab – a woman many would be inclined to discard. When God looked at Rahab, He didn't see a prostitute. He saw her faith. Rahab was spared along with her family, and these Gentiles went on to live among the Israelites.

But God's goodness does not end there.

Matthew 1:5 NIV tells us, "Salmon the father of Boaz, whose mother was Rahab."

The reason this verse in the book of Matthew is so important is because not only is Rahab labeled "mother," she is also named in the lineage of King David and Jesus Christ! This inclusion emphasizes God's redemptive plan extends to all, even those considered outsiders. Rahab is also one of the two women mentioned in Hebrews 11, a chapter often referred to as the "Hall of Faith" for its focus on exemplary figures who lived by faith.

Beloved, when Rahab stepped into salvation, she stepped out of her fear, shame, and her label. She was transformed and restored when she believed that the

God of Israel was worth trusting. Rahab was given a new name; she was called "mother" of Boaz and was welcomed lovingly into the family of Christ. She is still celebrated thousands of years later as a biblical heroine.

God wants to give you a new name today. But the only way He can do that is if you choose to decide the God of Israel is worth trusting. Step into salvation, or rededicate your life to the One who created you and reserves the right to name you. When you make this choice, you will begin the process of shedding the undesirable label or name that has weighed you down for far too long.

May we be fearless like Rahab!

PRAY WITH ME...

O God of Israel,

I long for the courage of Your daughter, Rahab. Grant me the strength to bravely shed the labels and names the world has placed upon me. I affirm that You are worthy of my trust, and I surrender my life to Your will. I confess my sins before You and open myself to Your healing touch. Lord, may Your transformative power work within me, in the name of Jesus.

Amen.

Day Fifty-Six

Meditation and Prayer: Father Sees You are More Than What Happened to You

*"A thief comes only to steal and kill and destroy. I
have come so that they may have
life and have it in abundance."*
John 10:10 CSB

When the brokenness of the world infiltrates our lives,
many of us grapple with doubts about God's kindness and the promise of a bright future. Trauma inflicted
by sexual violence, domestic abuse, addiction, grief, and
illness often leaves us questioning how a "good" God
could allow such suffering. It's natural to wonder if anything positive remains in store for us amidst such adver-

sity. Trauma often strips away our hope, joy, and peace, leaving behind deep despair.

Beloved, it is not enough for Satan to make sure that you have been hurt by the sin and wickedness he has caused in this world. He wants to finish you! Therefore, when you suffer, you can count on the devil digging his heels in and whispering more lies, more hurt, and more pain into your vulnerable ears.

Despair is like a dark labyrinth lined with trap doors set by the enemy. Each trapdoor hides a label he attaches to your spirit—"crazy," "loser," "damaged." Satan watches like a hungry lion, waiting for these labels to crush you. Then he strikes, whispering more lies, sending the wrong people your way, and reinforcing your sense of worthlessness with every blow.

If you choose to stay trapped, you pose no threat to his plans. Satan's goal is to steal your purpose, kill your spirit, and destroy your life. He works tirelessly to keep you defeated and dysfunctional.

Yet, there is hope! Where Satan sets traps, the Lord provides holy exit ramps. Jesus stands ready to guide you away from danger and onto a victorious path filled with peace and self-worth. *"He came so that you may have life and have it in abundance!"* He is the Beacon who lights your path to freedom and away from the trapdoors!

More good news: Jesus wants you to know that you are precious in His eyes, and He has a life-giving name to bestow upon you today. That name? "Child of the Most High God."

MEDITATION:

On this day of meditation and prayer, let's reflect on the simple yet powerful warning found in John 10:10. Let's enter the sanctuary of God's presence and encounter His perfect love.

Find a quiet place and get comfortable. Take a few deep breaths. Embrace the stillness around you, and declare that God is here with you. There is nowhere He would rather be.

Just breathe.

Now, picture yourself deep within the depths of a cavern, where darkness reigns. The faint echo of dripping water resonates softly in the distance, enveloping you in an eerie silence. The air is cool and thick, like a shroud of mist clinging to the shadows. Though unseen, the vast space around you feels intimidating. Carefully, you reach out and feel the rough texture of the cavern walls guiding you forward. With each step, fear and anticipation grow. You've been stumbling through this cavern for some time, and panic begins to seep into your body until a brilliant light emerges ahead, drawing you forward.

The brightness illuminates the walls of this underground passage, revealing the labels you've carried. They're carved into the rock, almost as deeply as the scars you have carried. Slowly turning a corner, you emerge into a beautiful clearing. Trees and flowers surround you, with a breathtaking waterfall in the distance. As you approach the water, the radiance that lit up the cavern reappears, and a blinding silhouette of Jesus walks toward you. It's hard to see Him clearly, but you catch a glimpse of His loving eyes. Instantly, you feel safe and cherished. He takes your hand and says:

"My beloved, I've been waiting for you. I'm proud of your steps of faith. Just as I brought light, I will bring your healing. I named you long ago, child. You are my masterpiece, and I love you. Now, let's spend some time together so you will finally know your worth."

PRAY WITH ME...

Jesus,

I want to shed my spirit of the names I have been called, the labels I settled for, and the identity I accepted. These are not from You, so I leave them at the foot of Your cross. I receive the names of purpose that You have just for me, Jesus. The enemy's schemes against me that were once in the darkness have come into the light, and I declare that Satan is defeated, in the name of Jesus. Thank You, Father, for deeming me worthy and making me Yours. I love you!

Amen.

Day Fifty-Seven

THE POWER OF GOD TO WORK IN OUR ANGER

Unresolved anger simmers in our souls — slowly eating away at our peace and joy like hydrochloric acid slowly burning its way through metal. Dr. Nadia says that life's disappointments, traumas, and injustices can leave us angry to the point of physical illness. She says, "Untreated and unsettled anger can impede our ability to heal from trauma. It prolongs the grieving process and undermines recovery from emotional wounds and addictions."

She added that anger can also cause physical illness, like high blood pressure, autoimmune disorders, insomnia, and even heart issues. Dr. Nadia said, "This is all the result of the chemicals and hormones being released in our bodies during episodes that trigger angry emotions.

Friends, anger is sinful unless you are dealing with righteous anger (John 2:13-18, 2 Samuel 12) that you are somehow channeling into change. Ongoing outrage eats away at us and has the power to destroy us. Anger over injustices inflicted upon us or others we care for is normal. Righteous indignation can also warn us when boundaries are violated and can help us protect ourselves. Not *all* anger is a sin. But when we refuse to let go of the rage we feel or refuse to work through it, we commit sin and cut ourselves off from God's peace and joy. The bottom line is this: you must deal with anger, or it will deal with you.

In the book of Numbers, Moses got angry at the Israelites, who complained about the lack of water in the desert. Frankly, they complained often and about a lot! Moses was fed up, and in his anger he disobeyed God, who gave him very specific commands for how to get water to his people. Moses acted out of anger and sinned, resulting in severe consequences.

"But the Lord said to Moses and Aaron, "Because you did not trust me enough to demonstrate my holiness to the people of Israel, you will not lead them into the land I am giving them!"
Numbers 20:12 NLT

Moses chose anger and forfeited his purpose! This is one of the saddest passages in all of the Bible. I know many of you reading these words have endured horrific things. How tragic would it be if you missed the very thing you were created for because of your anger and unwillingness to forgive?

Dear friend, let us not forget that our Compassionate Father is also a Righteous Judge. Who are we to try to assume His role? To allow for God's wrath is to handle anger biblically. I say this to you lovingly and gently, friend, for I know firsthand what it's like to stew in the anger of injustice.

Let us commit to working through anger. Here are some of the ways I was able to resolve this in my life:

1. Overcome evil with good (Romans 12:21). This is possible when we entrust our enemies to Jesus instead of trying to exact revenge. When we are obedient in this way, we look more like Jesus.

2. Work with a professional to deal with unsettled emotions. God has provided Christian counselors and therapists to help us work through the darkness of rage and resentment.

3. Confess your anger to Jesus, and share with Him just how hard this feels. He understands, and He will work on your heart.

4. Forgive. (Yes, I said the dreaded F-word.) To forgive is to say that we trust God to handle the evil that has touched us.

Beloved, this is hard work that can only be done with the help of the Holy Spirit. When we deal with anger this way, God can take what was meant to hurt us and use it for good, and we are liberated from the heavy chains of lingering resentment.

The Lord, in His tenderness, wants you to know that letting go of anger does not right the injustices, nor does it mean we must create relationships with those who have hurt us. Letting go simply means handing over our anger, hurt, and pain to the One who can right all wrongs.

Festering bitterness is a poison that can metastasize in your spirit and keep you from the presence of God. You, friend, are called to do big things in His name. Do not let malice disable you and keep you from your Promised Land. Get to the root of your outrage and claim the abundant life that has been declared over you, in Jesus' name!

Pray With Me...

Father,

I know there are things I am holding onto and simmering over. I am angry about what happened to me, to the one I love. If I am honest, I am angry at You, God. Please take this from me and forgive me. Give me Your heart of forgiveness, and allow me to see others through Your eyes of love and compassion. Lord, I hand over anger, resentment, bitterness, and blame. Have mercy on those who hurt me and heal my spirit. Remove my heart of stone, Lord, and give me a soft and responsive heart of flesh (Ezekiel 36:26), in the name of Jesus.

Amen.

Day Fifty-Eight

MEDITATION AND PRAYER: FATHER SEES YOUR ANGER AND DESIRES TO SET YOU FREE

"If it is possible, as far as it depends on you, live at peace with everyone. Do not take revenge, my dear friends, but leave room for God's wrath, for it is written: "It is mine to avenge; I will repay."
Romans 12:18-19 NIV

Today's scripture underscores that only God possesses the authority for wrath and vengeance. As the Creator of the universe and everything within it, only He holds the ultimate power to judge. Please understand, dear friend, I do not wish to diminish the pain inflicted on you, nor does this absolve anyone of responsibility. I strongly urge anyone who has suffered any form of violence to report perpetrators to the authorities and allow our justice system to take its course. Victims should also create boundaries that keep them safe.

I want to remind you that while Jesus is fully God, He is also fully man. He understands suffering and injustice deeply and is offended and enraged by it. Do you trust Him to hold wrongdoers accountable? Friends, we are called to surrender these emotions to Jesus, and we must remember that the devil is salivating at the chance to bind us with intense feelings of anger, bitterness, and resentment.

When you hold onto rage at those who wronged you, you build a wall between you and God. Haven't your perpetrators taken enough from you? Do not let them or the enemy have this victory too. Forgiveness takes time, so be patient with yourself. But if you pursue healing, God will meet you where you are and work on your vulnerable spirit.

Friends, forgiving the man who raped me was one of the hardest things I have ever done in my life. I never imagined I could do that, but I desperately desired freedom from my hatred, anger, pain, and shame. When I finally laid this all at the cross, God saw me and transformed my life.

My heart did not instantly change, but Papa was patient and ever so gentle with me. He tore down the altars that I built to my anger and resentment, one at a time, one day at a time. But I had to say the words and make the choice to forgive.

In my experience, forgiveness worked like a conduit that allowed healing waters to flow through me, and I experienced the true tenderness of a King who says, "No child, let Me. I've got you now." This is my wish for you. This is why I wrote these words. God has good plans for you, but first, He requires your trust and obedience.

MEDITATION:

On this day of reflection and devotion, let's take a moment to consider the healing wisdom of Romans 12. Together, let's step into God's sanctuary, where we can experience His gentle encouragement and the fullness of His presence.

Remove the distractions around you. Choose to open your heart and your spirit. Ask Father to speak to you. It's normal if your mind begins to wander. Just bring your thoughts back into this place. Keep your focus on King Jesus.

Be mindful of where you are sitting or lying right now. Can you feel any pent-up anger and frustration? Quietly identify the areas of your body carrying the rage. Breathe slowly and deeply.

Visualize yourself sitting in front of the ocean. You see turquoise water for miles. Waves are crashing against the shoreline, and seagulls are gliding through the air. But even with all this beauty, you sense the weight of the anger, resentment, and bitterness you have carried for so long.

Jesus takes His place on the sand beside you and whispers, "Give it all to Me, child."

You tearfully nod your head. Slowly, every emotion that has kept you stuck begins to detach from your spirit. On the sand around you, you see the words appear in bright red, "anger, resentment, rage, vengeance, bitterness, hatred." It's all there!

Jesus scoops up each emotion you have ever felt in his hands, and sand drips everywhere as he places it all inside a giant wooden crate beside Him.

Your eyes meet, and instantly, you feel His affection. There are no words to describe the love in His gaze. He closes the crate, locks it, and asks, "Are you ready, beloved?" You nod, and He effortlessly lifts the heavy crate, walks to the water, and tosses the crate into the deepest part of the sea. He walks back over and helps you up, and the two of you watch as the box drifts away and into the vast ocean.

"I am so very proud of you," says King Jesus.

Pray With Me...

God,

I am letting go of the burden of unforgiveness that has infected my heart. Lord, You know the pain and resentment that I've been carrying. Today, I humbly ask You to take it from me. Help me to forgive, as You have forgiven me. I trust that You have taken everything that was meant to destroy me, locked it up in that crate, and destroyed it at the bottom of the sea. I declare Your healing power is at work in me, and I receive every good thing You have in store for my life. I surrender unforgiveness to You. In Jesus' name, I pray.

Amen.

Day Fifty-Nine

THE POWER OF GOD TO HELP US FORGIVE THE UNFORGIVABLE

*"What a God we have! And how fortunate we are
to have Him, this Father of our Master Jesus! Because Jesus was raised from the dead, we've been
given a brand-new life and have everything to live
for, including a future in heaven—and the future
starts now! God is keeping careful watch over us
and the future. The day is coming when you'll have
it all—life healed and whole."*
1 Peter 1:3-5 MSG

Beloved brother, blessed sister, if our Creator could
defy the grave, could He not resurrect all that is dead
in your life? I say, "Yes," because I have seen it in my life
and the lives of so many others you have read about on
the pages of this devotional book!

If you've experienced trauma of any kind, I pray that you would understand that the Son of God, Jesus, allowed Himself to be tortured and put to death for this moment with you.

Jesus willingly experienced immense suffering to save you, friend. If you were the only person on earth, He still would have left the perfection of heaven to suffer through the pain and torture of the cross for you. That is how much our King loves you!

God longs to pour healing into your life. He desires to transform you from the inside and restore the years you've lost to pain and suffering. The Creator of the Universe did not make you in His image so you would live tortured on this side of the grave. But God has allowed us free will, and when Adam and Eve exercised that right and sinned in the Garden of Eden, nothing was ever the same again. In this world, we will have trouble, pain, and suffering. But that is not the end for you and me. Thanks be to God!

God's love is so profound and purposeful that He desires to transform the very thing the enemy intended to destroy you into a source of strength, wisdom, and greater likeness to Him.

Friend, we do not serve a cruel Papa who allows us to hurt for His selfish purposes — He uses our hurt, pain, and testimony of transformation to help others like us. In the darkest moments of our pain, He is closest to us, and in our deepest sorrows, we resemble Him. How can He let us fall? He won't! But we must cling tightly to Him.

Suffering in this life is not easy, I know. But getting to the other side of trauma is possible with faith in Christ, the courage to do what His Word says, the bravery to seek help, and the fervent desire to seek God in every part of this grueling and difficult recovery process.

Complete and perfect healing, permanent transformation, and absolute restoration await us in glory. But for now, we attach ourselves to the belief that all the good God has for us will be given to us "on earth as it is in heaven" (Matthew 6:10).

Pray With Me...

Blessed Father,

I believe that Your resurrection power is in me. I trust whatever You have planned for my story. Jesus, I am so sorry that You suffered the way You did and did so for me. Forgive me for my unbelief. I hand over my mustard-seed-size faith, and I ask You to fill me with the hope and expectation that You have an abundant life for me because You love me and want the very best for me.

Amen.

Day Sixty

Meditation and Prayer: Father Sees You and Calls You to Him

Jesus said, "I am the Bread of Life. The person who aligns with ME hungers no more and thirsts no more, ever. I have told you this explicitly because even though you have seen ME in action, you don't really believe ME. Every person the Father gives ME eventually comes running to ME. And once that person is with ME, I hold on and don't let go. I came down from heaven not to follow my own agenda but to accomplish the will of the One who sent ME."
John 6:35-38 MSG

O Beloved, I pray you would read this life-giving promise and believe! Jesus has drawn near to you as you have read these words. Over time, trauma has banished your spirit to a deeply lonely and barren desert.

But our Blessed Savior says you do not have to stay there, and if you take His hand today, He will ease your pain with His holy healing balm. He will replace your shame and guilt with His self-worth, self-respect, and the righteousness that comes from abiding in Christ.

Friend, our Precious Papa is good and kind, and He calls you to Himself. I dare you to take Him at His word, then stand back and watch in amazement as you witness His overhaul of your life.

MEDITATION:

Let us enter the presence of the Father of hope and healing. May we declare that He will mend our souls and make us whole.

Breathe in deeply and exhale slowly. Do this a couple more times. Then, when you are ready, read our final meditation, close your eyes, and invite the Holy Spirit to join you.

Today's scripture promises that once we are in the arms of our Holy Father, He never lets go of us. Picture Father holding you as He maneuvers through a dangerous minefield where sin and the devastation of trauma attempt to blow your legs out from underneath you. But our Protective Papa has swept you up, and He is walking right through the danger, unscathed and untouched, just like when He walked on water (John 6:16-21). That is what He does for you and me, friend.

Will you turn to Him now and take steps of faith toward your healing? The words in this book have been inspired by the One True God, who saved and restored me. I have prayed for you: the brokenhearted, the sick, addicted, and abused. Your hurt, pain, and shame has been written on my heart, and I have thought of you daily as I put these words to paper.

I want to leave you with this final message of hope. The Lover of your soul waits for you to call His name and invite Him into your sadness and despair. God wants to resurrect your life from the ashes of anguish. Choose the abundant life He died to give you.

Father holds His arms out to you now, invites you into His sweet embrace, and says, "I have always *SEEN* you, child. Just wait and see what I have for your life!"

PRAY WITH ME...

Almighty and Powerful God,

I love You. I adore You. I am in awe of You. I cannot fathom the depths of Your patience and kindness toward me. But I want all that You have for me. Today, I say "yes." I choose to follow You. I commit my life to You. I am determined to do the work, find the resources, and immerse myself in a church community and Your Word. I know I have a long road ahead, but with You by my side, I cannot fail. Here I am, Jesus, anoint my life and have Your will be done.

In the name of Jesus, I pray.
Amen.

A FINAL THOUGHT...

We have completed our journey together. You have read many powerful stories of believers who have seen God transform their lives from chaos to calm, and from pain to purpose. Now, you get to decide if you will be next. God has special plans for your future. He wants to restore all that your brokenness has taken from you.

He invites you to take His hand and embrace the adventure of a new life with El Roi, The God who sees you! Will you take a bold step of faith today and choose to trust Him if you haven't already? The tug you feel on your heart as you read this is the Holy Spirit drawing you to Him. Will you welcome Jesus into your life? Say "yes" and pray this final prayer with me, beloved.

Pray With Me...

Heavenly Father,

I have struggled for a long time. I have navigated life, especially trauma and brokenness, in my own way. I acknowledge my need for You and surrender my life to You, Savior.

I believe You are the Son of God, that You died on the cross for my sin, and that You rose from the dead, conquering darkness and death. I make You the Lord of my life. I invite You into my pain, depression, and anxiety. I ask You to begin the work of healing and transformation. Jesus, restore what I have lost.

I give You my past, my present, and my future. Help me to live for You and follow Your will all the days of my life. Strengthen my faith and help me to grow closer to You each day.

Thank You, Papa, for Your unfailing love and the gift of eternal life. I declare I am a new creation in You. In Your holy and precious name, I pray.

Amen.

LIFELINES

RAINN (RAPE, ABUSE, INCEST, NATIONAL NETWORK)

1-800-656-HOPE (4673)

www.rainn.org

SUICIDE AND CRISIS LIFELINE

Dial 988

SUICIDE PREVENTION LIFELINE

1-800-273-TALK (8255)

www.988lifeline.org

WONDHERFUL

If you know someone who is experiencing a mental crisis, is a recent suicide survivor, is grieving a family member of a recent suicidal crisis, or is suicidal, request a LIFE BOX at:

www.wondherful.com/lifebox

MIRANDA HEALING GROUP

The associates at The Miranda Healing Group are experts in counseling, with training from accredited institutions. Its team of qualified clinicians, each with specialized backgrounds, is dedicated to providing the highest level of care, both in person and through virtual sessions. They are ready to offer support in areas such as trauma, relational issues, grief, behavior modification, and Christian-based counseling.

7710 NW 71st Court, Suite 202, Tamarac, FL 33321

954-840-8583

MLRHealing.com

SAMHSA (SUBSTANCE ABUSE AND MENTAL HEALTH SERVICES ADMINISTRATION)

1-800-662-4357

www.samhsa.gov

REFERENCES

THE NEW STRONG'S EXPANDED EXHAUSTIVE CON-CORDANCE OF THE BIBLE. 2010. Red Letter Edition ed. Nashville, Tennessee: THOMAS NELSON.

www.ingramcontent.com/pod-product-compliance
Lightning Source LLC
Chambersburg PA
CBHW020823150626
46554CB00017B/1251